Prophecy - U

Helmut Silbach

New Wine Press
P.O. Box 17
Chichester PO20 6YB
England

Copyright © 1996   Helmut Silbach

All rights reserved. No part of this publication may be reproduced, stored in a retrieval system, or transmitted in any form, or by any means, mechanical, electronic, photocopying or otherwise, without the prior written consent of the publisher.

Short extracts may be used for review purposes.

Unless otherwise stated quotations are taken from
The King James Bible © Crown Copyright
and
The Holy Bible, New International Version
Copyright © 1973, 1978 International Bible Society.
Published by Hodder & Stoughton

ISBN 1 874367 51 5
Typeset by Tony MacCormack, Wilmslow, Cheshire
Printed in England by Clays Ltd, St Ives plc

Dedication

To my Dear Wife Rosemary

I dedicate this book to my wife and to all Christian wives who faithfully support the ministry of their husbands by taking over as much of the duties of life as possible. By thus doing they allow their husbands to devote more time to do the work of the Lord.

"Who can find a virtuous woman? for her price [is] far above rubies. .... Strength and honour [are] her clothing; and she shall rejoice in time to come. ... favour [is] deceitful, and beauty [is] vain: [but] a woman [that] feareth the LORD, she shall be praised."

Proverbs 31:10, 25 & 30

Prophecy - What Next ?
Helmut Silbach

And a voice came out of the throne, saying, Praise our God, all ye his servants, and ye that fear him, both small and great. And I heard as it were the voice of a great multitude, and as the voice of many waters, and as the voice of mighty thunderings, saying, Alleluia: for the Lord God omnipotent reigneth. Let us be glad and rejoice, and give honour to him: the marriage of the Lamb is come, and his wife hath made herself ready.

Revelation 19:5-7

Contents

Acknowledgements	9
Introduction	11

Part One
The Sequence of Last Day Events

The Order of the Last Day Events	15
For the Jew First 'The Olivet Discourse' ...	18
The 'Time of Jacob's Trouble'	20
Where the Eagles Gather	23
The Day of the Lord	30
The Days after Israel's Trouble	41
The Interval after the time of Jacob's Trouble ...	42
The Events at the End of Israel's Trouble ...	45
Also for the Greek 'Revelation'	59
The Lamb's Wrath upon the Nations	63
Revelation Chapter Seven	64
Revelation Chapter Eight	67
Revelation Chapter Nine	67
Revelation Chapter 10	68
Revelation Chapter 11	70
Events in That Day	73
- Angels Preach	76
- The City of Confusion	77
- The Treacherous Dealers...	79

Part Two
The Woman in the Sky

Who is the Woman of Revelation Chapter 12?...	85
The Two Wives in the Bible...	86
The Marriage of the Lamb	87
The Wife of Christ a Queen?	91
The Church in Psalm 45	95
Who is the Woman with the Man-Child of Revelation 12?	101
The Woman is Clothed with the Sun	104
The Woman has the Moon under her Feet ...	105
The Kingdom of Heaven	106
She Wears a Crown of 12 Stars	108
The Woman was with Child	109
A Great Red Dragon...	109
Satan the Great Horn	111
Why the Dragon want to Devour the Child ...	113
How the Dragon wants to Devour the Man-Child	114
The Child was Caught up to God and his Throne	115
The Other Man-Child	118
The Earth in Travail and Pain	125
The Woman in the Wilderness	128
War in Heaven	132
Satan and his Host	139
The Woman had Other Children	145
Israel in the Wilderness - A Type of Woman ...	146
Israel Does Not Represent the Woman of Revelation 12	153
Joseph's Dream	156
Can Mary be the Queen of Heaven?	157

Charts

Chart No 1
The Olivet Discourse in
Chronological Order 13

Chart No 2
Similarities between Ezekiel's
and John's Visions 62

Chart No 3
Table of Double Occurrences 72

Chart No 4
Scripture Comparison Chart 131

Chart No 5
All of Israel Compared with the
Woman in Heaven 147

Chart No 6
Israel in the Wilderness
Compared with the Woman in the Wilderness ... 148

Chart No 7
Israel's New Generation
Compared with the Man- Child 152

Foreword

The noted historian and internationalist JAMES T. SHORWELL recently observed:

"We are now at the last frontier, and in a sense, history must begin all over again. For it seems quite certain that we shall never again be even reasonably safe here on earth until all men without exception have become good men, or until God himself breaks once more into human history supernaturally - this time to establish with divine omnipotence a kingdom of righteousness and compassion upon earth, thus supplanting the misrule and impotence of men."

In this excellent book my good friend Helmut Silbach has, with typical German thoroughness, unveiled some knotty problems in the book of Revelation. For all of us who love the Lord, no matter how little or how much we understand the book of Revelation, we stand together, united and rejoicing in what we see to be the final outcome as given in chapter 16 verse 9:

"Alleluia, for the Lord God omnipotent reigneth"

The invincible King of Glory will have the last word in history.

"Now unto the King eternal, immortal, invisible, the only wise God, be honour and glory for ever and ever. Amen."

George T. Curle

Acknowledgements

George Curle — He was a great encouragement and help in getting this book published.

Russel Brown — May the Lord reward Russel for the help and inspiration he has given to me.

Stan Semenow — I thank Stan who installed the "ONLINE BIBLE" on my computer. This free program which was programmed by Christians for Christians was an excellent help in searching and copying Bible references.

Tony MacCormack — May the Lord bless this man who was willing to take on the task of preparing the manuscript for publishing this book from an unknown author.

My daughter Natasha — Thanks for her help in typing many of my hand written notes. Without that help it would have taken much longer to get the manuscript completed.

Introduction

" But thou, O Daniel, shut up the words and seal the book, even to the time of the end: many shall run to and fro, and knowledge shall be increased." (Daniel 12:4)

"But God has chosen the foolish things of the world to confound the wise; and God hath chosen the weak things of the world to confound the things which are mighty; ... That no flesh should glory in his presence." (1 Corinthians 1:27 & 29)

"But the anointing which ye have received of him abideth in you, and ye need not that any man teach you: but as the same anointing teacheth you of all things, and is truth, and is no lie, and even as it hath taught you, ye shall abide in him." (1 John 2:27)

The Bible declares that the word of prophecy cannot be fully understood until the time of the end. Furthermore, since the unlocking of prophetic events can only be done by the Holy Spirit, it follows that the wisdom of the world as taught in colleges and universities is not able to perform this task. But God has chosen the weak and foolish (as the world sees it), to declare his wisdom. The following pages are written in the hope that they will stimulate the desire of Christians to turn to the word of God in a humble and prayerful attitude, to study and search for themselves the depth of Scripture. There is much in God's word which has not yet been fully understood. There is much left to discover, all of which will be a help and comfort in today's wicked world.

God waits until his people approach him with the right attitude and desire, after that he will reveal additional truths hidden in his word, to guide and help those who seek him today. Since prophecy, until now, has been largely shut up, it would be futile to expect the key of understanding to be found in the learning institutions of the world, whether secular or religious. The Holy Spirit chose not to reveal these things to the wise of the world, since they would (as is true of man's nature) most likely claim the glory for themselves.

However there have already been many humble and Spirit filled men of man must have been Arthur E. Bloomfield. He provided the inspiration for Part Two of this study in chapters 12 to 16 of his book; 'ALL THINGS NEW'. He understood that the common view of Christians, who make the Woman of Revelation chapter 12 to be Israel, could not be right. Part Two of this study expands his view, namely that it must be the 'visible Church' and not Israel which is pictured by that woman.

Part One of this study uses segments out of the second part of the booklet; *'Bridge Over Troubled Waters' - 'That Unknown Time'*. Published October 1995, by Tony MacCormack, and distributed by New Wine Press, 22 Arun Business Park, Bognor Regis, West Sussex. PO22 9SX. England. Telephone (0)1243 867227. It is recommended to read that booklet, since it deals in greater detail with the subject of the time gap after the Tribulation.

It is also recommended to read this book *"Prophecy - What Next?"* through twice, to enable the serious student to obtain a fuller and deeper understanding of the issues under consideration.

Chart No 1 - The Olivet Discourse in Chronological Order

	Events in their Historical Setting	Where the Gospels Fit In		
		Matthew	Mark	Luke
AD 33	Jesus left the Temple. Disciples admire the Temple and ask three questions.	Chapter 24 verses 1-3	Chapter 13 verses 1-4	Chapter 21 verses 5-7
AD 33 to AD 68	But before all these things you will have persecution, beatings in synagogues, be cast into prison, accused before kings, delivered up by parents, friends and kinsfolk. Martyrdom. But in patience win your soul.			verses 12-19
AD 68 to AD 70	Jerusalem compassed, desolations at hand, flee to the mountains, days of vengeance, woe to them with child. They shall fall by the sword. Captive into all nations. Jerusalem trodden down by the Gentiles.			verses 20-24
Church Age	Deception. False christs. Wars and rumours of wars. Famine and earthquakes.	verses 4-6	verses 5-7	verses 8-9
Seven Years Tribulation	Beginning of travail. World wars, famines, earthquakes, tribulation. Hated by all nations Brother against brother.	verses 7-14	verses 8-13	verses 10-11
Tribulation Second Half	Abomination of desolation standing in the holy place. Jews in Judea flee into mountains. Don't delay your flight. Woe unto them with child. Great tribulation. False christs and false prophets show great signs. For the elect's sake those days will be shortened.	verses 15-28	verses 14-23	
Days after the Tribulation.	Sun and moon darkened. Stars falling from heaven. Powers of heaven shaken. Distress of nations. Perplexity because of roaring sea and billows. Men fainting for fear. Fearful of what is coming on the world. Sign of the Son of man appears. Son of man comes with power and great glory. Angels shall gather the elect Jews from earth and heaven.	verses 29-31	verses 24-27	verses 25-27
Judgment of the Gentile Nations	Christ shall sit on His throne in glory. Before Him all nations separated - sheep on His right hand, goats on His left hand. Jewish brethren before Him.	Ch 25:31 to 25:46		

Part One

The Order of the Last Day Events

There seems to be a general misconception, even amongst pre-tribulation Christians, regarding the sequence of last day events. But if the order of prophetic events is not clearly understood, the overall picture which one has cannot be correct either. Part One of this study endeavours to briefly outline how the events of the last days, according to the Scriptures, will unfold. This author believes that Scripture must be read and interpreted in a plain literal manner, and that the Old and New Testaments present one harmonic picture. The word of God is constructed like a jigsaw puzzle in order that the unbeliever or casual reader will not understand. But a complete picture will emerge if the Holy Spirit guides the searching heart. Interpreting Scripture in a literal manner does not mean that one denies that the word of God uses symbols. However these symbols will never contradict other passages which can be understood using the plain literal method.

Here then is an outline of events, as the Bible seems to show them.

1. The rapture of the true Church.

2. The first half of Israel's Tribulation, and the war of the serpent against the woman's seed.

3. The second half of Israel's Tribulation - the Great Tribulation - the time of Jacob's trouble.

4. The day of the Lord's wrath.

5. The Lord's second coming.

6. The millennium.

Point One:

We shall not investigate the rapture itself. However it will be referred to during the study of other points, and it should become clear that indeed the rapture will have to come first in the prophetic calendar.

Points Two to Six:

Will be explained by using the Olivet discourse and the first few chapters of Revelation as a framework.

But first some preliminaries. It is important to the understanding of prophecy that we always consider the context of the whole passage, plus the setting and circumstance when the prophecy was made. For example, when the Lord prophesied on the mount of Olives, in Matthew 24, the prophesy was in response to three questions by his disciples. The Lord had just spoken about the coming destruction of the Jewish temple and Jerusalem. What then was the motive of the disciples in asking those questions? It has been stated:

'The Jews, including the pious, held to a coming of the Messiah, the literal restoration of the Davidic throne and Kingdom, the personal reign of Messiah on David's throne, the resultant exaltation of Jerusalem and the Jewish nation, and the fulfilment of the Millennial descriptions of that reign. It is also acknowledged, that the utterances of Luke 1:71; Act 1:6, Luke 2:26, 30 etc., include the above belief, and that at least until the day of Pentecost, the Jews, the disciples, and even the apostles, held such a view.... they regarded the prophecies and convenanted promises as literal, (i.e. in their naked grammatical sense); and, believing in the fulfilment, looked for such a restoration of the Davidic Kingdom under the Messiah, with an increased power and glory befitting the majesty of the predicted King... " **(Theocratic Kingdom, I;** Page 183 G.N.H. Peters)

The Lord himself never dashed their hopes, he had announced the fact that the kingdom was at hand.

"After the termination of the ministry of the herald (John the Baptist Matthew 4:12), the Lord began his public ministry with the announcement: 'Repent: for the kingdom of heaven is at hand' (Matthew 10:7), the seventy are sent forth and the command is given: "say unto them, the Kingdom of God is come nigh unto you." (Luke 10:9,11)..... By the term "at hand" the announcement is being made that the Kingdom is to be expected imminently." **(Things to Come;** Page. 449 J.D. Pentecost)

That the predicted literal Jewish Kingdom was indeed at this stage at hand, is further proven by the remarks of our Lord in Matthew 23:37 when he said: *"O Jerusalem, Jerusalem, thou that killest the prophets, and stonest them which are sent unto thee, how often would I have gathered thy children together, even as a hen gathereth her chickens under her wings, and ye would not."*

We can see by these passages alone that the Jews and disciples rightfully expected that the Lord would usher in their much anticipated Kingdom. What would have happened to the Church if Israel had repented is known only by God and we should not speculate on it. However, that does not change the fact that the kingdom of God was offered to them, **then and there.**

How great must have been the disappointment of the disciples when the Lord, in Matthew chapters 23 and 24, predicted the coming destruction of Jerusalem during that generation. This must have been a great shock to them, especially when he shortly afterwards spoke in detail about the destruction of their beloved temple. It is therefore easy to understand their concern and why they asked Jesus, in Matthew 24:3 about the future of their beloved homeland. For this reason they came privately (Matthew 24:3) asking the Lord what the future would bring for Israel, and when he would come to usher in their Kingdom.

Would our Lord shock them by speaking about the Gentile Church, a thing which at this stage they could not comprehend? All they were interested in was the future of Israel, our Lord answered their questions point by point. The whole programme that was unfolded before them was totally in relation to Israel, both for the believing and unbelieving Jew. Let us not fall into the same trap that Jewish and Christian generations have fallen into, by assuming that the word of God revolves around their generation, or that the Church is the end of all, and that Israel no longer holds an important place in the plan of God. It is true that the Bible portrays two pictures of the kingdom of God: The literal and the spiritual. Nevertheless, it should be realised that in Matthew 23 and 24 the context demands a literal interpretation. There are just too many references to literal persons, actions, buildings, cities, countries, etc., all in Israel. For this reason the context here clearly demands an interpretation for a literal Jewish Kingdom. More on this subject later.

For the Jew First
'The Olivet Discourse'

The Olivet discourse will be briefly explained, as given by Matthew, Mark and Luke. Thereafter it will be compared with the first half of the book of Revelation.

After announcing the destruction of Jerusalem and the temple, the Lord was asked three questions by the disciples in Matthew 24:3:

1. **When shall Jerusalem by destroyed?**

2. **What shall be the sign of thy coming?**

3. **What shall be the sign of the end of the age?**

The Lord Jesus answers first question two, then question one, followed by question three. All three accounts start by giving a brief description of the years leading up to the Tribulation. Which is the time we today know as the Church Age. However the Lord did not refer to the Church, that section of the discourse closed with the statement, *"But the end is not yet."* Matthew 24:3-6, Mark 13: 3-7 and Luke 21:7-9. This is followed, in all three accounts, by an overview of the seven Tribulation years. It should be noted that each of the three gospel writers places a different importance, and emphasises a different aspect of this area.

When the Lord Jesus gave that prophecy he formulated it in such a way that it had a double application. The time of travail he spoke of covered both the time up to and including 70AD and also the seven tribulation years. The three gospel writers on the other hand, under inspiration, wrote only what suited their theme. Therefore Matthew wrote his account of that section mainly with the tribulation in view (Matthew 24:7-14). Refer to Chart One **'The Olivet Discourse in Chronological Order'** on page 14.

Matthew starts as do all three, by referring to a coming world war or wars, plus famines and earthquakes, which mark the beginning of the Tribulation. He concludes that section with the remark *"and then shall the end come"*. The end here refers to the coming of the Lord.

Luke starts in the same way as Matthew, by describing the signs which mark the beginning of the Tribulation Luke 21:10. He finishes that section in verse 11 by referring to the signs in heaven, which mark the end of the tribulation (compare Matthew 24:29). He then states clearly in Luke 21:12, *"but before all these things"*, thus indicating that he switches back from the end of the Tribulation to a previous time segment. The context makes it clear that he now records the Lord's answer to the first question, the destruction of Jerusalem and the time leading up to it. From verse 12 to 19 he explains the situation before 70AD. Verses 20 to 24 deal with the time around 70AD when God's wrath fell upon that generation and the Romans destroyed Jerusalem and the Jewish nation. He concludes that passage by stating that Jerusalem will be *"trodden down by the Gentiles until the time of the Gentiles be fulfilled"* (verse 24). Thus terminating that section with a reference to the end of the Tribulation.

Mark also starts that section by quoting the signs which indicate the start of the Tribulation (Mark 13:8-13). Nation against nation etc. But unlike Matthew who continued with a description of the Tribulation, and unlike Luke who primarily described the Jewish situation up to 70AD, Mark writes his account as a mixture. Some events describe the period up to 70AD, others the situation during the Tribulation. Thus his account has a double application.

However by reading all three accounts it becomes evident that history turns a full circle. The situation during the Tribulation is very much like the time before 70AD with one important difference; when persecuted in the first century, Israel never repented, but when they are persecuted during the Tribulation they finally will repent.

One point before moving on. Matthew 24:14 states that *"the gospel of the kingdom shall be preached in the whole world and then shall the end come"*. This gospel is the preaching of the coming kingdom. The gospel of the '**kingdom**' is different from the Christian gospel. One proclaims the coming kingdom, and the need for repentance, Matthew 10:7 and Luke 9:2-3. The other proclaims the way of salvation by grace 1 Corinthians 15:1-4.

Luke, after describing briefly the Tribulation in 21:10 & 11, never again refers to it, yet Mark and Matthew do, by explaining in greater detail what happens during the second half.

After giving an outline of the Tribulation as described above, Matthew and Mark thereafter focus on the time after the middle of the Tribulation. This section includes Mark 13:14-23 and Matthew 24:15-28. They describe in greater detail the time of the **'Great Tribulation'**, after the setting up of the abomination which causes desolation. The first half of the Tribulation will also witness the war of the serpent against the remnant of the woman's seed, the tribulation saints. It is during this time that Satan persecutes those which have been left behind at the rapture. For an in-depth study on this subject refer to Part Two.

The 'Time of Jacob's Trouble'

It should be explained that there is a difference between a tribulation and the day of the Lord's wrath. A tribulation, regardless if it is for the Jew or Gentile, is a time designed by God to lead his chosen, either Jew or Gentile to repentance. While the day of the Lord is a time of wrath.

Let us continue by looking at the word **tribulation**.

"For then shall be great tribulation, such as was not since the beginning of the world to this time, no, nor ever shall be." (Matthew 24:21)

What is the meaning of this verse? The first mention of the word tribulation is found in Deuteronomy 4:30. Where Israel is told that they will have tribulation in the latter days. Hence according to the law of first mention, we can connect the word tribulation with sinful Israel, unless the context demands otherwise. The same is implied in Judges 10:14, where Israel is said to be in tribulation because of sin. Likewise the time of Jacob's trouble, Jeremiah 30:4-8, describes a day of unprecedented trouble for Israel and Judah, a time none like it. And in Daniel 9:27 it is also stated that Israel will experience a time of trouble as never before, a prophecy to which our Lord referred in his Olivet discourse. In order to fully comprehend the Olivet discourse and then other scriptural prophecies, we should first understand at what time in human history the following Scriptures are to apply.

Deuteronomy 4:30-31; *"When thou art in tribulation, and all these* things are come upon thee, even in the latter days, if thou turn to the Lord thy God, and shalt be obedient unto his voice: (For the Lord thy God is a merciful God;) he will not forsake thee."

Jeremiah 30:4-8; "And these are the words that the Lord spake concerning Israel and concerning Judah. For thus saith the Lord; We have heard a voice of trembling, of fear, and not of peace. Ask ye now, and see whether a man doth travail with child? wherefore do I see every man with his hands on his loins, as a woman in travail, and all faces are turned into paleness? Alas! for that day is great, so that none is like it: it is even the time of Jacob's trouble; but he shall be saved out of it. For it shall come to pass in that day, saith the Lord of hosts, that I will break his yoke from off thy neck, and will burst thy bonds, and strangers shall no more serve themselves of him:"

Daniel 9:27; "And he shall confirm the covenant with many for one week: and in the midst of the week he shall cause the sacrifice and the oblation to cease, and for the overspreading of abominations he shall make it desolate, even until the consummation, and that determined shall be poured upon the desolate."

Daniel 11:31; "And arms shall stand on his part, and they shall pollute the sanctuary of strength, and shall take away the daily sacrifice, and they shall place the abomination that maketh desolate."

Daniel 12:1; "And at that time shall Michael stand up, the great prince which standeth for the children of thy people: and there shall be a time of trouble, such as never was since there was a nation even to that same time: and at that time thy people shall be delivered, every one that shall be found written in the book."

Matthew 24:15-16 & 21; "When ye therefore shall see the abomination of desolation, spoken of by Daniel the prophet, stand in the holy place, (whoso readeth, let him understand:) Then let them which be in Judea flee into the mountains: For then shall be great tribulation, such as was not since the beginning of the world to this time, no, nor ever shall be."

It is evident that right through the Old Testament the prophets of old warned about a coming time of unprecedented trouble for the nation of

Israel, which should be expected in the latter days. Moses in Deuteronomy 4:30 mentions it, Jeremiah in Jeremiah 30:4-8 refers to it, Daniel states the same, a time of trouble such as never was, since there was a nation, which indicates that this trouble or tribulation is for the nation of Israel. The Lord refers to Daniel's end time prophecy by connecting the Great Tribulation of Matthew 24:15 & 21 to Daniel's time of trouble. Consequently it can be concluded that the great tribulation mentioned in the Olivet discourse, will be a time of trouble for the nation of Israel, it is the time of Jacob's trouble. This term is a better description than 'great tribulation', since it specifically points out that the trouble is for Israel. There are other times of great trouble mentioned in the word of God. But that period mentioned in Matthew 24 refers to Israel's time of great trouble as predicted by the prophets. Hence in this study, we shall frequently use the term '*the time of Jacob's trouble*'. That time will be so bad, that if God would not shorten those days, no Jew, whether elect or not, would survive. There will also be a time of great trouble for the Gentiles, as mentioned in Revelation, but that time will be autonomous from '*the time of Jacob's trouble*'.

Matthew 24:22; *"And except those days should be shortened, there should no flesh be saved: but for the elect's sake those days shall be shortened."*

The word shorten denotes 'to cut off', 'amputate', 'curtail', 'shorten' (ref. **'Expository Dictionary'** by W.A. Vine). The meaning of that verse is, that God will bring that Great Tribulation to a sudden stop. When Satan is in full flight, trying to exterminate that nation once and for all, God will intervene and cut off that time of trouble. The Lord himself will break the yoke of Antichrist from off the neck of Jacob - Jeremiah 30:8. Or as Daniel writes "*at that time thy people shall be delivered*" . Daniel 12:1.

Hence it can be concluded that the main purpose of the Tribulation is to lead Israel to repentance. Once that has happened, the Tribulation has served its purpose and will be terminated. This does not mean that the time of trouble for the rest of the world finishes at the same time. Remember for the Jews first and also for the Greeks. Therefore calamity starts first for the Jews and also finishes first for them and after that starts the day of the Lord's wrath for the Gentiles. This explains why in Mark 13:24 and Matthew 24:29 the Tribulation is said to have finished, yet the trouble for the world is far from over. It has ended for the Jews, they are no longer under the judgement of God

Now the time of 3½ years given to Antichrist is his time of dominion over Israel. It does not have to mean that he will come to his end immediately after Israel's Tribulation has ended. Rather he will be cast into hell at the time of the Lord's return.

Daniel 12:1; *"And at that time shall Michael stand up, the great prince which standeth for the children of thy people: and there shall be a time of trouble, such as never was since there was a nation [even] to that same time: and at that time thy people shall be delivered, **every one** that shall be found written in the book."*

Matthew 24:22; *"And except those days should be shortened, there should no flesh be saved* (saved can mean: to rescue from danger or destruction): *but for the elect's sake those days shall be shortened."*

In Daniel it is stated, that all those Jews who are written in a certain book shall be delivered during the time of Israel's great Tribulation (delivered means also; escape or save). The parallel passage in Matthew informs us that if those days would not be cut off, no Jew would survive, they would all die. Consequently if we read both passages in conjunction then it would appear that all the elect Jews are saved from death. Every Jew who belongs to God will come through this time. This would mean that not one of the elect Jews will be killed during those days. Hence we must not expect to find any Jew amongst the Tribulation saints in heaven. Michael will make sure that the elect will live through that horrible time.

Before the time of the interval is considered, the difficult statements in Luke 17:37 and Matthew 24:28 have to be explained.

Where the Eagles Gather

There are two passages in Scripture where our Lord speaks about the eagles gathering. One is in Luke 17:37, the other in Matthew 24:28. At first glance they appear to have the same meaning, but at a closer look it will be discovered that they are set in a different context and in a different time. Let's first investigate the text in Luke.

Scripture indicates that at the time of the second coming of the Lord Jesus Christ the world, and Israel, will be divided into the saved and the lost. A separation will take place. Both Jew and Gentile will be divided into saved and lost. The saved will enter into the millennium, while the lost will be cast into Hell or Hades. The Lord will cleanse his kingdom from all unbelievers. This will be performed in the spiritual realm (Zechariah 13:2) and also in the physical. At the start of the millennium, the world will be absolutely free from all unbelievers.

This collecting of the Jews from all over the world is indicated in Luke 17:34 & Matthew 24:28. The Lord here speaks to Jews about Jews. He states that at the time of his coming two will be in bed, thus indicating that it is night. But also two men shall be in the field, obviously working, which in those days was only possible at day time. Therefore since the same event happens while it is night at one place, but day at another, it shows that two different locations in the world must be in view. Thus a gathering of the elect from all over the world is indicated.

Mark 13:27; *"And then shall he send his angels, and shall gather together his elect from the four winds, from the uttermost part of the earth to the uttermost part of heaven."*

Matthew 24:31; *"And he shall send his angels with a great sound of a trumpet, and they shall gather together his elect from the four winds, from one end of heaven to the other."*

These two passages speak about the same event and confirm the above statement. Here is it clearly stated that our Lord will send forth his angels to collect the elected Jews from all over the world. Only the saved will be collected and taken to Israel, the unbelieving Jews will not be taken to safety. This gathering of the elect is also mentioned in Isaiah 27:12-13:

"And it shall come to pass in that day, that the Lord shall beat off from the channel of the river unto the stream of Egypt, and ye shall be gathered one by one, O ye children of Israel. And it shall come to pass in that day, that the great trumpet shall be blown, and they shall come which were ready to perish in the land of Assyria, and the outcasts in the land of Egypt, and shall worship the Lord in the holy mount at Jerusalem."

Note that it is stated that the Jews were ready to perish **before** they were gathered one by one. They were ready to perish during the Tribulation, but now after they have been gathered, they are safely in Jerusalem and worship the Lord. Which indicates again that the gathering of the Jews follows after Jacob's time of trouble.

Also here as in Matthew it is stated that a trumpet will be blown and that the children of Israel will be gathered one by one. Clearly the same event is in view, which shows that the elect which will be gathered by the angels from all over the world are saved Jews. These Jews are the brethren of our Lord to whom he refers in Matthew 25:40 & 45. They will all be taken to Israel and afterwards stand by the Lord, as he judges the nations following Israel's tribulation.

In the Olivet discourse (Mark 13:27, and Matthew 24:31), the Lord mentions the angels gathering the elect of Israel. This gathering of the elect is also referred to in Luke 17:26-36, and in the parallel passage in Matthew 24:37-41. These scriptures speak about the same event. The Lord would hardly refer to the gathering of the elect in Matthew 24:31, and then ten verses later in Matthew 24:40-41, reverse the order by making those which are taken to be the wicked. This fact is made clearer by reading together the two parallel passages in Luke 17:26-36 and Matthew 24:37-41. The Lord first speaks about the situation in Noah's and Lot's days. He states that immediately after the families of Noah and Lot were taken to safety, death and destruction fell upon those which were left behind. Hence those taken were taken to safety. While those left behind were destroyed. Immediately following the description of what happened in Noah's and Lot's days, the Lord declares in Luke 17:30, and Matthew 24:37 and 39, *"Even thus shall it be in the day when the Son of man is revealed."* Thus, revealing that those which are taken will be the elect which are taken to safety. While those left behind are the wicked which have to face death.

If it is only the elect Jews who are gathered by the angels, what will happen to those who are not elected and are left behind? The destiny of the wicked is foretold in Matthew 25:26 & 30:

"His Lord answered and said unto him, Thou wicked and slothful servant, thou knewest that I reap where I sowed not, and gather where I have not strawed: ... And cast ye the unprofitable servant into outer darkness: there shall be weeping and gnashing of teeth."

The Lord continues in his Olivet discourse to explain to the Jews what the future would bring for them. As was explained before, the Olivet discourse was given mainly for the benefit of the Jews. Therefore the servants here are Jews. The slothful servants are unbelieving Jews, who will be cast into Hell. This is confirmed in Matthew 8:12 and Matthew 24:51:

"But the children of the kingdom shall be cast out into outer darkness: there shall be weeping and gnashing of teeth."

"And shall cut him asunder, and appoint him his portion with the hypocrites: there shall be weeping and gnashing of teeth."

Matthew 24:51 states the same fact. But who are those who are commanded in Matthew 25:30 to perform the act of casting the unbelievers into Hell. The Lord commanded "Cast Ye", who are the "**Ye**"? They must be angels, since in another prophecy which speaks about the end of the world or age, that is at the end of the millennium, the angels will again perform such a cleansing operation. This is recorded in Matthew 13:40-42:

"As therefore the tares are gathered and burned in the fire; so shall it be in the end of the world. The Son of man shall send forth his angels, and they shall gather out of his kingdom all things that offend, and them which do iniquity. And shall cast them into a furnace of fire: there shall be wailing and gnashing of teeth."

Here the angels collect the wicked and cast them into Hell. This then seems to be one of the duties of angels. The angels are God's servants, they do whatever the Lord commands them. They protect the godly (Psalm 34:7; 91:11-12), inform the elect (Acts 10:22), and collect the elect and the wicked etc., but they can also kill if so commanded. Remember the army of the Assyrians and the citizens of Jerusalem (2 Kings 19:35; 1 Chronicles 21:12-18). Angels can also carry the soul of a dead person to Abraham's bosom (paradise) Luke 16:22. Therefore the unbelieving Jews which have not been gathered together by the angels, will be left to face judgement. They will die, just as the wicked outside the ark, or inside Sodom died, while the just were taken to safety. The angels of the Lord will take them and cast them alive or dead into hell or hades. For the wicked, the angels will be angels of death. If this fact is kept in mind then it will be easier to understand the difficult statement of our Lord in Luke 17:37; *"And they answered and said unto him, Where, Lord? and he said unto them, Wheresoever the body is, thither will the eagles be gathered together."* The best way to understand this prophecy is by looking first at the context and setting of the whole passage.

Luke 17:22-26; *"And he said unto the disciples, the days will come, when ye shall desire to see one of the days of the Son of man, and ye shall not see [it]. And they shall say to you, See here; or see there: go not after [them], nor follow [them]; for as the lightening, that **lighteneth** out of the one [part] under heaven, **shineth** unto the other [part] under heaven, so shall also the Son of man be in his day. But first must he suffer many things, and be rejected of this generation. And as it was in the days of Noe, so shall it be also in the days of the Son of man."*

In Luke 17:22-23; the Lord speaks about the time during Israel's seven Tribulation years, when the Jews desire to see the Messiah come to help them. False leaders will appear to mislead the Jews. The Lord warns his people not to be mislead nor to be deceived by them. Since his appearing will be as bright as lightning, his coming and appearance cannot be faked. The Lord explains the conditions just before he will appear as King to introduce his kingdom. He tells his disciples how the wicked in the days of Noah and Lot were all concerned with the cares of daily living until the day of judgement. Those left outside the ark, and those inside Sodom all died. Following this the Lord speaks about the separation of the elect and the wicked.

Two are together in bed (probably husband and wife, the word 'men' as written in the King James version is not in the original), one will be taken, the other left. Again two are in the field, only one will be accepted. The emphasis here is on a selective separation which takes place all over the world at the same time. The disciples who kept quiet until now, at this point interject with a question. "**Where, Lord?**" Why the question? They seem to have understood everything until now, so why that question at this point. Could it be that they were confused about the statement about two sleeping at night while at the same time two were working in the field? If they were, then their question makes sense. They inquired where this would take place. They could not understand that Jews could be working at night in the field. Such a thing was unknown in those days. Then the Lord answers them, where all this will take place. *"wheresoever the body is, thither will the eagles be gathered together."*

The word for '**body**' here in the Greek is 'soma' which denotes '**a sound whole**'. It does not denote a carcase as in Matthew 24:28. Therefore a complete body is here in view, this body may be alive or dead. But if dead, then it would not have started to decompose.

The eagle is a bird of prey, *"They are passed away as the swift ships: as the eagle that hasteth to the prey"* (Job 9:26). *"Doth the eagle mount up at thy command, and make her nest on high? She dwelleth and abideth on the rock, upon the crag of the rock, and the strong place. From thence she seeketh the prey, and her eyes behold afar off."* (Job 39:27-29)

The eagle is also a swift hunter which swoops down on its victim, to carry it away. It also gathers where the slain are. (Job 39:30) The picture is that of a swift hunter which grabs its prey by surprise to carry it to destruction, and which gathers where the slain are to be found. It was already indicated that the elect of Israel will be collected by the angels and brought to Israel to meet the Lord. But it was also pointed out that the wicked will be cast into hell. We have already seen that angels are to perform that duty. Consequently it seems reasonable to assume that the eagles represent the death angels of the Lord, who seek out all those wicked Jews who have been left behind. The Lord answers his disciples, that wheresoever the angels find one or more of the wicked in the world, that is where they will gather to take them and cast them into Hell. Since the world will have to be cleansed from all unbelievers before the Lord ushers in his kingdom.

The other passage where the gathering of the eagles is mentioned is Matthew 24:28, there the context demands a different interpretation. The context in Matthew 24 speaks about the danger of following false christs and false prophets. These are out to deceive the Jews, even the very elect. To counteract this, the Lord explains to the Jews how to be on their guard against these false christs and false prophets. They will be able to clearly judge any claim of messiahship by comparing the way in which that prophet was revealed with the sign foretold in Scripture. The true Christ will come shining as lightning. As lightning shines from one end of the sky to the other, so will be the coming of Christ. When the Lord appeared to Paul on the Damascus road his light was so brilliant that Paul was blinded. It is the same light in which the Lord will suddenly make his entry into the affairs of Israel at the end of the Tribulation. The Lord will come to help the Jews, and to terminate the great Jewish Tribulation. This arrival to help the Jews after Israel's time of trouble, is not the same as when he will appear later, with all his saints, to officially introduce the Kingdom of God.

When the Lord comes to help Israel, he will come to the mount of Olives to fight for them (Compare Zechariah 14:3-5). When he comes to usher in the millennium, he will come with his saints in the clouds of heaven. He will come after the whole world has for some time seen his sign in the sky (Matthew 24:30). His coming will be slow and majestic with power and glory. The tribes of the earth will have time enough to understand that the time for them is up, and they will mourn. There is therefore a marked difference between the appearing of the Lord in Mark 13 and in Matthew 24. This fact, together with the different context of the passages, makes it clear that two different interpretations are required.

Matthew 24:26-28; *"Wherefore if they shall say unto you, Behold, he is in the desert; go not forth: behold, he is in the secret chambers; believe it not. For as the lightning cometh out of the east, and shineth even unto the west; so shall also the coming of the Son of man be. For wheresoever the carcase is, there will the eagles be gathered together."*

The Lord explains what not to do and what not to believe. Then in verse 27 he says *"For"*, he draws a contrast between the appearance of the false christs and his own appearing. He emphasises the difference between them and himself.

The next verse (28) also starts with the word '**For**'. The purpose for it must be the same as in the previous verse, namely to show the Jews how to recognise the false christs and prophets. They can also recognise the impostors by their eagle like actions. The eagle is known as a swift hunter, but he will also feast on a carcase if the opportunity should arise. The carcase in this context must by the spiritually dead body of Israel during the Tribulation. That a group of people can be seen as being spiritually dead is indicated in Matthew 8:22, and

Revelation 3:1. The false christs and false prophets will come to feed on a religious carcase, which has died a long time ago. This already happens today in the Christian world, where multitudes of false teachers feed on the carcase of apostate Christianity. This will be repeated in Israel during the Tribulation. Only the very elect will not fall for their deception.

The Day of the Lord

At this stage of the study it must be explained that the '**Great Tribulation**' and the '**Day of the Lord's Wrath**' are not the same. 'The Day of the Lord' or 'The Day of the Lord's or Lamb's Wrath' refer to the time when God's wrath and anger will primarily be poured out on an unbelieving and anti-Semitic Gentile world. It is God's response to the hatred of the Gentile nations against the Jews, his chosen people. It is the revenge for which the persecuted Jews have always asked. However, God could never avenge his people as long as they remain in sin and unbelief. God has to permit the persecution to go on unhindered until the Jews repent and turn to Jesus Christ for help. This is the purpose of the time of Jacob's trouble. But as soon as Israel acknowledges that Christ is their Lord the Tribulation will have served its purpose. Then God will act, and Christ will fight for his people and intervene on their behalf. (Zechariah 14:3-4)

We now investigate the Scriptures which bear this out, always keeping in mind that God's wrath is directed against the Gentile unbelievers. But there is also a time of great trouble (tribulation) for the Gentiles, which serves the same purpose. That tribulation is independent from Jacob's time of trouble, and is also different from the day of God's wrath. The great tribulation for the Gentiles probably starts some time after the beginning of Israel's Tribulation and is referred to in the book of Revelation.

But we will analyse Scriptures dealing with the day of the Lord. The phrase "The day of the Lord" can be found 25 times in the Bible. It is a time when God's wrath will fall on the wicked and unbelievers. Israel already experienced their 'day of the Lord', which occurred when the Babylonians ransacked the land of the Jews. Remember '*for the Jew first, but also for the Greek*'. Therefore whenever the word of God (after the Babylonian captivity) in a prophetic context, speaks about "the day of the Lord" it always relates to the Gentiles. "The day of the Lord", and related expressions connect the wrath of God with the unbelieving Gentiles.

Isaiah 2:12-21 *"For the day of the LORD of hosts [shall be] upon every [one that is] proud and lofty, and upon every [one that is] lifted up; and he shall be brought low: And upon all the cedars of **Lebanon**, [that are] high and lifted up, and upon all the oaks of **Bashan**, And upon all the high mountains, and upon all the hills [that are] lifted up, And upon every high tower, and upon every fenced wall, And upon all the ships of **Tarshish**, and upon all pleasant pictures. And the loftiness of man shall be bowed down, and the haughtiness of men shall be made low: and the LORD alone shall be exalted in that day. And the idols he shall utterly abolish. And they shall go into the holes of the rocks, and into the caves of the earth, for fear of the LORD, and for the glory of his majesty, when he ariseth to shake terribly the earth. In that day a man shall cast his idols of silver, and his idols of gold, which they made [each one] for himself to worship, to the moles and to the bats; To go into the clefts of the rocks, and into the tops of the ragged rocks, for fear of the LORD, and for the glory of his majesty, when he ariseth to shake terribly the earth."* (Compare with Revelation 6:15)

This is the passage where the expression "The day of the LORD" appears for the first time in the Bible. Consequently this verse, according to the law of first mention, gives us a clue to understand all other Scriptures where the same phrase is used. The first time when a word or expression is mentioned in the Bible will provide the key to the understanding of all other Scriptures where the same subject is to be found. Therefore in the passage above, we are informed that the day of the Lord is directed against all the proud and haughty of the world. Hence we can expect all other Scriptures where the same term is used, to give us further information how God is going to deal with unrepentant men. The text here indicates that " the day of the Lord" is directed against Gentile nations. This is a clue which will be helpful when similar passages are considered.

Isaiah 13:6-11; *"Howl ye: for the day of the LORD [is] at hand; it shall come as a destruction from the Almighty. Therefore shall all* *hands be faint, and every man's heart shall melt: And they shall be afraid: pangs and sorrows shall take hold of them; they shall be in pain as a woman that travaileth: they shall be amazed one at another; their faces [shall be as] flames. Behold, the day of the LORD cometh, cruel both with wrath and fierce anger, to lay the land desolate: and he shall destroy the sinners thereof out of it. For the stars of heaven and the constellations thereof shall not give their light: the sun shall be darkened in his going forth, and the moon shall not cause her light to shine. And I will punish the **world** for [their] evil, and the wicked for their iniquity; and I will cause the arrogancy of the proud to cease, and will lay low the haughtiness of the terrible.*"

Once more the context indicates that "The day of the Lord" is directed against the wicked and evil of the world (the Gentiles). It is a time of punishment. In comparison a tribulation, regardless of whether for Jew or Gentile, is a time to bring God's chosen in repentance to Jesus Christ.

Isaiah 34:2-8; "*For the indignation of the LORD [is] **upon all nations**, and [his] fury upon all their armies: he hath utterly destroyed them, he hath delivered them to the slaughter. Their slain also shall be cast out, and their stink shall come up out of their carcases, and the mountains shall be melted with their blood. And all the host of heaven shall be dissolved, and the heavens shall be rolled together as a scroll: and all their host shall fall down, as the leaf falleth off from the vine, and as a falling [fig] from the fig tree. For my sword shall be bathed in heaven: behold, it shall come down upon **Idumea**, and upon the people of my curse, to judgment. The sword of the LORD is filled with blood, it is made fat with fatness, [and] with the blood of lambs and goats, with the fat of the kidneys of rams: for the LORD hath a sacrifice in **Bozrah**, and a great slaughter in the land of Idumea. And the unicorns shall come down with them, and the bullocks with the bulls; and their land shall be soaked with blood, and their dust made fat with fatness. For [it is] the day of the LORD'S vengeance, [and] the year of recompences for the controversy (for the cause) of Zion.*"

The Lord's indignation is against the nations of the world. The reason for this is vengeance against those who oppressed Israel. God will take up the cause of his people.

Jeremiah 46:9-11; *"Come up, ye horses; and rage, ye chariots; and let the mighty men come forth; the **Ethiopians** and the **Libyans**, that handle the shield; and the **Lydians**, that handle [and] bend the bow. For this [is] the day of the Lord GOD of hosts, a day of vengeance, that he may avenge him of his adversaries: and the sword shall devour, and it shall be satiate and made drunk with their blood: for the Lord GOD of hosts hath a sacrifice in the north country by the river Euphrates. Go up into Gilead, and take balm, O virgin, the daughter of Egypt: in vain shalt thou use many medicines; [for] thou shalt not be cured."*

Again the day of vengeance against the Gentile nations is predicted.

Ezekiel 13:5; *"Ye have not gone up into the gaps, neither made up the hedge for the house of Israel to stand in the battle in the day of the LORD."*

This is one of two places where the term "the day of the Lord" relates to Israel. But since this passage is not prophetic in context, but deals with past events, the principle mentioned before is not violated.

Ezekiel 30:1-3; *"The word of the LORD came again unto me, saying, Son of man, prophesy and say, Thus saith the Lord GOD; Howl ye, Woe worth the day! For the day [is] near, even the day of the LORD [is] near, a cloudy day; it shall be the time of **the heathen**."*

Unmistakenly this prophetic passage is referring to "the day of the Lord" and connects the heathen (Gentiles) to the wrath of God.

Joel 1:14-16;

Verse 14; *"Sanctify ye a fast, call a solemn assembly, gather the elders and all the inhabitants of the land into the house of the Lord your God, and cry unto the Lord."*

Verse 15; *"Alas for the day! for the day of the Lord is at hand, and as a mighty destruction from the Almighty shall it come."*

Verse 16; *"Is not the meat cut off before our eyes, yea, joy and gladness from the house of our God?"*

Verse 14 calls for Israel's repentance and help from the Lord. Verse 15 announces the coming of the Day of the Lord which will bring destruction upon the enemies of Israel. Verses 16 to 20 lament Israel's condition during the Tribulation, and give the reason why the Day of the Lord is justified.

Joel 2:1 & 11; Verse 1; *"Blow ye the trumpet in Zion, and sound an alarm in my holy mountain: let all the inhabitants of the land tremble: for the day of the Lord cometh, for it is nigh at hand;"*

Verse 11; *"And the Lord shall utter his voice before his army: for his camp is very great: for he is strong that executeth his word: for the day of the Lord is great and very terrible; and who can abide it?"*

The call goes out to blow an alarm on the trumpet. Because the day of the Lord is now at hand Israel must prepare itself for refining and purging. The inhabitants of the land will include all those Gentile nations occupying the vast land of Israel, they must tremble. The day of the Lord is coming and he will deal with those who hate Israel and occupy their land. That day will be dark and gloomy, full of clouds of smoke. A description of a part of the warfare during that time is given. In verse 11 the direct intervention of the Lord is recorded. Nobody but those trusting in Christ shall survive.

Joel 2:30-32. *"And I will shew wonders in the heavens and in the earth, blood and fire, and pillars of smoke. The sun shall be turned into darkness, and the moon into blood before the great and the terrible day of the LORD come. And it shall come to pass, [that] whosoever shall call on the name of the LORD shall be delivered: for in mount Zion and in Jerusalem shall be deliverance, as the LORD hath said, and in the remnant whom the LORD shall call."*

Please take note of the difference here. The sun and moon will be turned into darkness before *"that **great** and **terrible** day of the LORD"*. But not before *"the **day** of the Lord"*. The day of the Lord starts when the sun and the moon will be darkened, while that **terrible day** comes later. That this great and terrible day of the Lord is not directed against Israel is made clear by the context.

Joel 3:1-3. *"For, behold, in those days, and in that time, when I shall bring again the captivity of Judah and Jerusalem, I will also gather all nations, and will bring them down into the valley of Jehoshaphat, and will plead with them there for my people and [for] my heritage Israel, whom they have scattered among the nations, and parted my land. And they have cast lots for my people; and have given a boy for an harlot, and sold a girl for wine, that they might drink.*"

In those days the Lord will avenge his people.

Joel 3:12-17. "*Let the **heathen** be wakened, and come up to the valley of Jehoshaphat: for there will I sit to judge all the heathen round about. Put ye in the sickle, for the harvest is ripe: come, get you down; for the press is full, the fats overflow; for their wickedness [is] great. Multitudes, multitudes in the valley of decision: for the day of the LORD [is] near in the valley of decision. The sun and the moon shall be darkened, and the stars shall withdraw their shining. The LORD also shall roar out of Zion, and utter his voice from Jerusalem; and the heavens and the earth shall shake: but the LORD [will be] the hope of his people, and the strength of the children of Israel. So shall ye know that I [am] the LORD your God dwelling in Zion, my holy mountain: then shall Jerusalem be holy, and there shall no strangers pass through her any more.*"

The call goes out to the Gentiles to get ready for war. God is waiting to judge them. When the sun and moon will be darkened, then the day of the Lord begins. The Lord will first come to the mount of Olives to help his people, and from there he will wage war against the Gentiles, he then will enter the temple (**which will be on mount Zion**), to purify the sons of Levi. The Lord will roar out of Zion with a loud voice and the saints of Israel are raised (refer to the chapter "**The Other Man-Child**" in Part Two). The reaping of the wicked in the valley of Jehoshaphat is also mentioned in Isaiah chapter 24 and in Revelation chapter 14 verses 17-20; and will be considered in the chapter "**The Treacherous Dealers**".

Amos 5:18 & 20

Verse 18; "*Woe unto you that desire the day of the Lord! to what end is it for you? the day of the Lord is darkness, and not light.*"

Verse 20; "*Shall not the day of the Lord be darkness, and not light?*

even very dark, and no brightness in it?"

God warns those Jews who desire the day of the Lord. Some Jews may desire that day because God's wrath falls upon the Gentiles. However that attitude is wrong. Again the darkness and gloominess of that day is mentioned.

Obadiah 15; *"For the day of the Lord is near upon all the heathen: as thou hast done, it shall be done unto thee: thy reward shall return upon thine own head."*

Here is one of the clearest descriptions for the purpose of the day of the Lord. It's main purpose is to bring revenge upon the heathen or Gentiles. Their wickedness will be returned upon their own head.

Zephaniah 1:14-18; *"The great day of the Lord [is] near, [it is] near, and hasteth greatly, [even] the voice of the day of the Lord: the mighty man shall cry there bitterly. That day is a day of wrath, a day of trouble and distress, a day of wasteness and desolation, a day of darkness and gloominess, a day of clouds and thick darkness. A day of the trumpet and alarm against the fenced cities, and against the high towers. And I will bring distress upon men, that they shall walk like blind men, because they have sinned against the LORD: and their blood shall be poured out as dust and their flesh as the dung. Neither their silver nor their gold shall be able to deliver them in the day of the Lord's wrath; but the whole land shall be devoured by the fire of his jealousy: for he shall make even a speedy riddance of all them that dwell in the land."*

This is the second passage where Israel is mentioned in connection with a day of the Lord. The time of that prophecy is about 625BC, several years before the Babylonian captivity. The context from verse four to verse 13 speaks about Israel's sin of idolatry and Baal worship.

Zephaniah 2:1-3. *"Gather yourselves together, yea, gather together, O nation not desired: Before the decree bring forth, before the day pass as the chaff, before the fierce anger of the Lord come upon you, before the day of the Lord's anger come upon you. Seek ye the Lord, all ye meek of the earth, which have wrought his judgement; seek righteousness, seek meekness: it may be ye shall be hid in the day of the Lord's anger."*

Luther in his German translation translates the phrase *"O nation not desired"* as **"hostile nation"** a translation which fits the context better. The hostile Gentile nation (or nations) will face the fierce anger of the Lord. But even so, those amongst the Gentiles who seek the Lord may be protected even during those horrible days. But it appears that they have to repent before the great day of the Lord's anger starts, because it is possible that during the day of the Lord only wrath comes down from heaven. The heathen would have the opportunity for repentance during the time of great trouble (or tribulation) which also comes for the Gentiles.

Zechariah 14:1-3; *"Behold a day is coming for the Lord when the spoil taken from you will be divided among you. For I will gather all nations against Jerusalem to battle, and the city will be captured, the houses plundered, the woman ravished, and half of the city exiled, but the rest of the people will not be cut off from the city. Then the Lord will go forth and fight against those nations, as when he fights on a day of battle."* (New American Standard Bible, reference Edition 1973).

In this instance, the usually reliable text in the King James Bible; *"Behold the day of the Lord cometh"* does not seem to be correct. Luther who is also reliable, translates this phrase similar to the New American Standard Bible, therefore that text is quoted. This gathering of all nations against Jerusalem must happen during the Great Tribulation, not after it. The fact that one day "all nations" will come against Jerusalem does not surprise a Christian who knows prophecy The growing hostility by the United Nations against Israel, may soon lead to the situation where the United Nations will feel compelled to invade Jerusalem.

Joel 2:31; *"The sun shall be turned into darkness, and the moon into blood, before the great and the terrible day of the Lord come."*

Zechariah 14:6-7; *"And it shall come to pass in that day, that the light shall not be clear, nor dark: But it shall be one day which shall be known to the Lord, not day, nor night: but it shall come to pass, that at evening time it shall be light."*

In these verses the day of the Lord is once more described. The same signs as before are mentioned, darkness, and gloominess. The day of the Lord is a period of time. However, 'the great and terrible day' must be a specific day inside the day of the Lord. At the start of the day of the Lord, there must be world-wide fires and volcanic eruptions. The result will be an enormous amount of smoke and ash in the atmosphere, which will cause the sun to be darkened and the moon will look like blood. Afterwards an atomic holocaust will break upon the world. This would represent the **'great and terrible day of the Lord'**. To understand these verses they must be read in conjunction with Isaiah 24:1, & 19-20, where it is stated that the earth will be turned upside down and that the earth will reel to and fro like a drunkard. Obviously the earth's axis will be turned around, perhaps because of many bombs all exploding at once at the same place, or because of the impact of a giant meteorite smashing into the earth. The earth will not immediately stabilise, but will wobble for a while. This wobble would cause the dark and light periods of the day to be thrown out of order. Therefore at daytime when it used to be light it will now be dark, and what used to be night, will now have some form of light. This must be what Zechariah 14:7 describes. This process could continue for a long time, perhaps for the whole period which is known as the day of the Lord. The order, duration, and appearance of day and night will be thrown into total confusion.

Malachi 4:1-3; *"For, behold, the day cometh, that shall burn as an oven; and all the proud, yea, and all that do wickedly, shall be stubble: and the day that cometh shall burn them up, saith the Lord of hosts, that it shall leave them neither root nor branch. But unto you that fear my name shall the Sun of righteousness arise with healing in his wings; and ye shall go forth, and grow up as calves of the stall. And ye shall tread down the wicked; for they shall be ashes under the soles of your feet in the day that I shall do [this], saith the LORD of hosts."*

Again the destruction of the wicked through fire (atomic bombs?) is described. It is a fact of history, that whatever weapon man invented, sooner or later he has used it. The day of the Lord seems to describe the effects of many atomic blasts. This is also indicated in Joel 2:30; "pillars of smoke", is a good description of exploding atom bombs. But for the Jews who have by now repented, the dawn of a new age is on the horizon, full of righteousness. However, it will not be the 'Age of Aquarius' as is expected by the New Age movement.

Malachi 4:5-6; *"Behold, I will send you Elijah the prophet before the coming of the great and dreadful day of the Lord and he shall turn the heart of the fathers to the children, and the heart of the children to their fathers, lest I come and smite the earth with a curse."*

Here we have some more details regarding the time of the day of the Lord.

In Revelation 11:3-12, the actions of the two witnesses who are generally understood to be Moses and Elijah, are recorded (compare also with Matthew 17:10-11). Note, it is stated that, **before that day comes**, Elijah the prophet will be sent. Consequently if the great day of the Lord and the Tribulation were one and the same event, then those two witnesses of Revelation chapter 11 would have to appear on the scene **before** the Tribulation. This scenario is clearly impossible. But if those witnesses appear during the time of Jacob's trouble which comes before the day of the Lord, then Scripture harmonises.

1 Thessalonians 5:1-4; *"But of the times and the seasons, brethren, ye have no need that I write unto you. For yourselves know perfectly that the day of the Lord so cometh as a thief in the night. For when they shall say, Peace and safety; then sudden destruction cometh upon them, as travail upon a woman with child; and they shall not escape. But ye, brethren, are not in darkness, that that day should overtake you as a thief."*

The wicked of the world will expect peace and prosperity, but suddenly the day of the Lord breaks upon them. Note; it does not say that there is peace, they only expect it to come.

2 Thessalonians 2:1 & 2; *"Now we beseech you, brethren, by the coming of our Lord Jesus Christ, and by our gathering together unto him, That ye be not soon shaken in mind, or be troubled, neither by spirit, nor by word, nor by letter as from us, as that the day of Christ is at hand."*

Paul exhorts the Thessalonians not to be troubled, not to panic. Why were they shaken in mind? Well they assumed that the day of Christ was very close, and this terrified them. They must have therefore understood the difference between the time of Jacob's trouble and the day of the Lord, because the Tribulation brings no fear to the Christian who believes in the pre-tribulation rapture. He knows that he will be taken out of the world before the Tribulation. But if someone could convince him that inside a few weeks the sun and moon would be darkened and that the powers of heaven would be shaken, then no doubt he would be troubled. That Christian would have to assume that the day of God's wrath was just around the corner, and that he therefore was already inside the Tribulation. He missed the rapture which meant that he was not saved at all. Certainly this scenario would trouble any Christian.

For that reason Paul had to comfort those Thessalonians, by explaining to them that the Day of Christ could not possibly be upon them. First of all two events had to come to pass:

1. The apostasy.

2. The revealing of the Antichrist.

That the apostasy comes first is understood by all. But if the Tribulation and the day of Christ are one and the same event, then there is something amiss here. According to verse three Antichrist has to be revealed **before** that day comes. Now if both the Tribulation and the day of Christ are identical, then Antichrist would have to come before the Tribulation. But according to Daniel 9:27, Antichrist will confirm a convenant with Israel for seven years, he will break this covenant 3½ years later; that act according to Matthew 24:15 & 21 is the start of the time of Jacob's trouble, it begins the second half of the seven year Tribulation period for Israel. This means that the first half must start 3½ years earlier at the time when the covenant is confirmed when Antichrist is revealed. But Paul says that he will be revealed before 'that day'. Obviously 'that day' therefore cannot refer to the Tribulation, since the Tribulation starts after Antichrist is revealed. But it can refer to the day of the Lord, because that day comes after the Tribulation and after the revealing of Antichrist. It is therefore concluded that the passage in 2 Thessalonians 2:1-8 confirms that the day of the Lord must come **after** the time of Jacob's trouble.

2 Peter 3:10; *"But the day of the Lord will come as a thief in the night; in the which the heavens shall pass away with a great noise, and the elements shall melt with fervent heat, the earth also and the works that are therein shall be burned up."*

The great day of the Lord will come suddenly and unexpectedly.

Having established that the Day of the Lord comes after the Great Tribulation. Let us now investigate those days as described in the Olivet discourse.

The Days after Israel's Tribulation

Matthew 24:29; *"Immediately after the tribulation of those days the sun shall be darkened, and the moon shall not give her light, and the stars shall fall from heaven and the powers of the heavens shall be shaken."*

Mark 13:24; *"But in those days, after that tribulation the sun shall be darkened, and the moon shall not give her light, and the stars shall be falling from heaven."*

Here are the predicted heavenly signs which mark the end of the Tribulation but the start of the day of the Lamb's wrath (Revelation 6:16-17), as discussed before.

In these verses it is stated that Israel's Tribulation has terminated. But please note that the troubles for the world continue. However Israel no longer has to suffer the wrath of God. They have repented and now enjoy God's protection. But for the world the day of wrath has arrived. The rest of the Olivet discourse describes the day of wrath from Israel's perspective.

Matthew 24:30; *"And then shall appear the sign of the son of man in heaven: and then shall all the tribes of the earth mourn, and they shall see the Son of man coming in the clouds of heaven with power and great glory."*

Matthew does not mention *'The days **after** the tribulation'* as is written in Mark 13:24, but straight away records the sign of the Son of man. This sign is probably the same as 'His Star' which was seen by the men from the east. That the star could not have been a literal star should be obvious, since no literal star can stand over a house. It was more likely the 'Glory of The Lord' which used to fill the house of God (2 Chronicles 5:14) which they saw on this occasion, and was named '**His Star**'. If so, then '**His Star**' appeared at his first coming and will also appear at his second coming. *'The sign of the Son of man'* (note: it is not called the sign of his coming), could perhaps, just as his star, be seen for several months prior to his coming. From the first sighting of the star by the men from the east, until they arrived at Joseph's and Mary's house, there must have passed several months, perhaps even two years. In those days it would have taken them that long to prepare and execute such a journey. This may be an indication of the duration of the time interval between the end of Israel's trouble and the coming of the Lord with his saints.

The Interval after the Time of Jacob's Trouble

As shown in the previous chapter there are days after Israel's Tribulation which no longer belong to the Tribulation and are separate from it. They form an interval between the close of the Tribulation for Israel and the coming of the Lord in the verse following.

Matthew 24:30; *"And then shall appear the sign of the Son of man in heaven and then shall all the tribes of the earth mourn, and they shall see the Son of man coming on the clouds of heaven with power and great glory."*

But the sign of the sun and moon being darkened signifies more than the end of Israel's Tribulation, it also heralds the start of the great day of the Lamb's wrath (Revelation 6:16-17). Therefore it is very important to notice that the word of God makes a clear distinction between '**the time of Jacob's trouble**' which serves to lead Israel to repentance, and '**the Day of the Lamb's wrath**' which is the wrath of God on an anti-

Semitic and wicked Gentile world. The Tribulation is that period of time as specified by Daniel in Chapter 9 verses 24 to 27. It is the time of Jacob's trouble, and it will also bring to an end '**the Time of the Gentiles**' mentioned by the Lord. Notice the sequence: Beginning with verse 29 the day of the Lord starts, it is **then** that the sign of the Son of man appears. It does not state that the sign must follow immediately after the beginning of the day of the Lord. There can be an unknown length of time between the two events. Likewise the next event, the coming of the Son of man. This too can happen at any time after the appearance of the sign. Therefore these two events can span the whole period of the day of the Lord.

Daniel 9:24-25; *"Seventy weeks (that is seventy periods of seven) are determined upon thy people and upon thy holy city, to finish the transgression, and to make an end of sins, and to make reconciliation for iniquity, and to bring in everlasting righteousness, and to seal up vision and prophecy, and to anoint the most Holy. Know therefore and understand, that from the going forth of the commandment to restore and to build Jerusalem unto the Messiah the Prince shall be seven weeks, and threescore and two weeks:"*

This shows that 70 sevens less 69 sevens until Jesus Christ offered himself as King leaves one seven, i.e. seven years are left until all these things which are written here are fulfilled. *"And he (*Antichrist*) shall confirm the covenant with many for one week: and in the midst of the week he shall cause the sacrifice and the oblation to cease, and for the overspreading of abomination he shall make it desolate, even until the consummation (*completion*), and that determined shall be poured upon the desolate"* (Daniel 9:27).

Daniel 12:1; *"And at that time shall Michael stand up, the great prince which standeth for the children of thy people: and there shall be a time of trouble, such as never was since there was a nation to that same time: and at that time thy people shall be delivered, every one that shall be found written in the book."*

Hence the event mentioned here is the same as the one in Matthew 24:15 to 21 and in Daniel 9:27 etc. This tells us that from this point onwards to the end of the time of trouble, or the Tribulation, there will be precisely 1,260 days. Note, regardless of all the trouble, those Jews who belong to God will be saved - that is, they will not die. For the Church, a heavenly people, the Lord uses the rapture to get them safely to heaven, but for Israel, God's earthly people, he uses other means to protect them here on earth.

Daniel 12:6-7; *"How long shall it be to the end of these wonders? And I heard the man clothed in linen, which was upon the waters of the river, when he held up his right hand and his left hand unto heaven, and sware by him that liveth forever that it shall be for a time, times, and a half:* (for three and a half prophetic years) *and when he* (Antichrist) *shall have accomplished to scatter the power of the holy people, all these things shall be finished."* >>**1260 days**<<

It will be 3½ prophetic years, or 1,260 days to the end, when all will be finished. Note, stating that it will take three and a half years until the end of Israel's tribulation has been reached, is the same as saying that from the middle of their tribulation **(when the abomination is set up)** until the end of it, will be 1,260 days. Once more it is confirmed that after 1,260 days the Tribulation for Israel will come to an end.

Daniel 12:11-12; *"And from the time the daily sacrifice shall be taken away, and the abomination that maketh desolate set up, shall be a thousand two hundred and ninety days. Blessed is he that waiteth, and cometh to the thousand three hundred and five and thirty days."* **1,290 days and 1,335 days.**

Now note: We have already seen that from the setting up of the abomination until the end of the time of Jacob's trouble there will be 1,260 days, yet here we have a period of 1,290 days from the setting up until an unknown event. Therefore this event goes 30 days past the Tribulation already indicating an interval. But since there are 1,335 days mentioned, from the midpoint until some other event, there has to be a **minimum** time interval of 75 days between the end of the Tribulation and the coming of the Lord in glory.

But since nobody knows the day nor hour of Christ's return. it could very well be more than 75 days. This would explain why the 10 virgins fall asleep while waiting for the Lord to return.

By studying those verses which deal with the end time, one is tempted to speculate what those unidentified events could be. At the end of the following chapter an attempt will be made to identify those events.

44

The Events at the End of Israel's Trouble

Having shown that there exists an interval of time after Israel's trouble and the coming of the Lord in glory, we now investigate the sequence of events in those days.

Mark 13:8-9 & 12-13; *"For nation shall rise against nation, and kingdom against kingdom: and there shall be earthquakes in divers places, and there shall be famines and troubles: these [are] **the beginnings of sorrows.** But take heed to yourselves: for they shall deliver you up to councils; and in the synagogues ye shall be beaten: and ye shall be brought before rulers and kings for my sake, for a testimony against them. ... Now the brother shall betray the brother to death, and the father the son; and children shall rise up against [their] parents, and shall cause them to be put to death. And ye shall be hated of all [men] for my name's sake: but he that shall endure unto the end, the same shall be saved."*

These verses describe the beginning of Israel's Tribulation. It appears that at that time the rulers of Israel will still be unbelievers; they will persecute those who after the rapture have come to a saving knowledge of Christ. Perhaps Israel's leaders, just as today, try to appease those world rulers who are sold out to the anti-Christian New Age movement. But it will not work, and soon Israel's great tribulation will come upon them.

Daniel 12:1; *"And at that time shall Michael stand up, the great prince which standeth for the children of thy people: **and there shall be a time of trouble, such as never was** since there was a nation [even] to that same time: and at that time thy people shall be delivered, **every one** that shall be found written in the book."*

It is certain - and a very important point to remember - that none of the very elect of Israel will die. Because Michael and later the Lord Jesus himself will protect the elect even during that time. The fact that this time is called "the time of Jacob's trouble" implies even that much. Jacob **(supplanter)**, before his name was changed to Israel **(God prevails)**, is generally understood to represent the un-converted part of that nation. Hence those which are betrayed and put to death may very well be the unbelievers, or the religious Jews. Consequently we should understand that the elect of Israel will all survive that time. For this reason we will not find any Jew amongst those various groups of Tribulation saints as they are mentioned in the book of Revelation. This fact confirms that the book of Revelation relates mainly to the Gentiles.

Matthew 24:21-22; *"For then shall be great tribulation, **such as was not since the beginning of the world to this time, no, nor ever shall be**. And except those days should be shortened, there should no flesh be saved but for the elect's sake those days will be shortened."*

The time of Jacob's trouble will be cut off, for the deliverance of the elected Jews.

Daniel 12:7; *"And I heard the man clothed in linen, which [was] upon the waters of the river, when he held up his right hand and his left hand unto heaven, and sware by him that liveth for ever that [it shall be] **for a time, times, and an half; and when he shall have accomplished to scatter the power of the holy people, all these [things] shall be finished**."*

Daniel 12:11; *"**And from the time [that] the daily [sacrifice] shall be taken away, and the abomination that maketh desolate set up, [there shall be] a thousand two hundred and ninety days**."* (3½ years).

Israel's great Tribulation will last for 3½ years. It starts from that point of time when the abomination is set up, and will end after Israel's repentance.

Matthew 24:15-16; *"When ye therefore shall see the abomination of desolation, spoken of by Daniel the prophet, stand in the holy place, (whoso readeth, let him understand:) Then let them which be in Judea flee into the mountains:"*

The Jews who are in Israel (there are others throughout the world) are admonished to flee to safety. But since most Jews at that time still don't believe in Christ, most will not adhere to his warning.

Zechariah 14:1-2; "*Behold a day is coming for the Lord when the spoil taken from you will be divided among you. For I will gather all nations against Jerusalem to battle, and the city will be captured, the houses plundered, the women ravished, and half of the city exiled, but the rest of the people will not be cut off from the city.*" (NASB Reference Edition 1973)

It is during Israel's great Tribulation that the nations (**the United Nations**?), will capture Jerusalem.

Matthew 23:39; "*For I say unto you, Ye shall not see me henceforth, till ye shall say, Blessed [is] he that cometh in the name of the Lord.*"

Jeremiah 30:7-8; "*Alas! for that day [is] great, so that none [is] like it: it [is] even the time of Jacob's trouble; but he shall be saved out of it. for it shall come to pass in that day, saith the LORD of hosts, [that] I will break his yoke from off thy neck, and will burst thy bonds, and strangers shall no more serve themselves of him:*"

It will be at that time right at the end of Israel's great Tribulation, that Israel (perhaps her leaders), will in utter desperation call out to the Lord Jesus for help. This act will terminate the time of Jacob's trouble, and the day of the Lord, with his darkness and gloominess, will start immediately.

Matthew 24:29; "*Immediately after the tribulation of those days shall the sun be **darkened**, and the moon shall not give her light, and the stars shall fall from heaven, and the powers of the heavens shall be shaken.*"

The Lord will return to precisely the same spot from where he left the earth 2,000 years ago, when he ascended to heaven; namely, the mount of Olives.

Acts 1:11-12; "*Which also said, Ye men of Galilee, (note, the address is to the men of Galilee, that is to all Jewish believers and unbelievers alike) why stand ye gazing up into heaven? this same Jesus, which is taken up from you into heaven, shall so **come in like manner** as ye have seen him go into heaven. Then returned they unto Jerusalem from the mount called **Olivet**, which is from Jerusalem a sabbath day's journey.*"

47

The Lord left from the mount of Olives which is east of Jerusalem and will return to it. But take note; he will '**come in like manner**'. The word of God means exactly what it states. The Lord will come back to the mount of Olives in the same way as he left. He left from that mountain, he will return to that mountain. Some Jews (**they were not yet Christians**) saw him rise up, some Jews will see him come down. It was a cloudy day when he left, it will be a cloudy day when he comes. He rose up **alone** all by himself, he will come back **alone** all by himself. This fact that the Lord rose alone gives us the key to distinguish between his different appearances. According to Scripture the Lord will leave heaven at least three times during those days. First he will call out his Church while he remains in the air, he will not descend to the earth. Thus that coming is clearly distinguished from his appearing on the mount of Olives. Secondly he returns alone to the mount of Olives. And thirdly he comes **with all his saints** (1 Thessalonians 3:13 & Jude verse 14) not alone, to usher in God's kingdom. Thus Scripture demands a minimum of three appearances of our Lord during that time.

1 Thessalonians 3:13; *"To the end he may establish your hearts unblameable in holiness before God, even our Father, at the coming of our Lord Jesus Christ with **all his saints**."*

Matthew 28:3; *"His countenance was like lightning, and his raiment white as snow:"*

When the Lord will appear on that mount he will be as bright as lightning.

Matthew 24:27; *"For as the lightning cometh out of the **east**, and **shineth** even unto the west; so shall also the coming of the Son of man be."*

The emphasis here is on the light and the direction of a lightning, not on its speed. The Lord will appear in brilliant light east of Jerusalem, his light will shine to Jerusalem which is west of the mount of Olives, where he will descend. He will descend slowly, for all to see, unmistakably.

Luke 17:24; *"For as the lightning, that **lighteneth** out of the one [part] under heaven, shineth unto the other [part] under heaven; so shall also the Son of man be in his day."*

Again the emphasis is on the light of a lightning. The days immediately after that Tribulation will be dark and gloomy, a fitting scenario for the time when Satan is in control. But the appearance of the Lord Jesus will be a stark contrast to those dark days. A brilliant light in a dark world.

Zechariah 14:3-5; *"Then shall the LORD go forth, and fight against those nations, as when he fought in the day of battle. And his feet shall stand in that day upon the mount of Olives, which [is] before Jerusalem on the east, and the mount of Olives shall cleave in the midst thereof toward the east and toward the west, [and there shall be] a very great valley; and half of the mountain shall remove toward the north, and half of it toward the south. And ye shall flee [to] the valley of the mountains; for the valley of the mountains shall reach unto Azal yea, ye shall flee, like as ye fled from before the earthquake in the days of Uzziah king of Judah."*

The Lord will fight from the mount of Olives which will split in two, to provide an escape from the fighting for the Jews. Thereafter Antichrist and his forces will be thrown out, and Jerusalem shall be liberated.

Malachi 4:5-6; *"Behold, I will send you Elijah the prophet before the coming of the great and dreadful day of the LORD: And he shall turn the heart of the fathers to the children, and the heart of the children to their fathers, lest I come and smite the earth with a curse."*

Before the Lord enters into Jerusalem Elijah will have restored the situation in Jerusalem; that is, he will have prepared the heart of his people for repentance. But the earth, after that event, will be cursed; that is, the day of the Lord's wrath will break upon it.

Matthew 17:10-11; *"And his disciples asked him, saying, Why then say the scribes that Elias must come first? And Jesus answered and said unto them, Elias truly shall first come, and restore all things."*

John the Baptist was a type of Elijah, but the real Elijah will appear to prepare the way before the Lord. The Lord comes at the end of Israel's tribulation.

Malachi 3:1-6; *"Behold, I will send my messenger, and he shall prepare the way before me: and the Lord, whom ye seek, shall suddenly come to his temple, even the messenger of the covenant, whom ye delight in: behold, he shall come, saith the LORD of hosts. But who may abide the day of his coming? and who shall stand when he appeareth? for he [is] like a refiner's fire, and like fullers' soap: And he shall sit [as] a refiner and purifier of silver: and he shall purify the sons of Levi, and purge them as gold and silver, that they may offer unto the LORD an offering in righteousness. Then shall the offering of Judah and Jerusalem be pleasant unto the LORD, as in the days of old, and as in former years. And I will come near to you to judgment; and I will be a swift witness against the sorcerers, and against the adulterers, and against false swearers, and against those that oppress the hireling in [his] wages, the widow, and the fatherless, and that turn aside the stranger [from his right], and fear not me, saith the LORD of hosts. For I [am] the LORD, I change not; therefore ye sons of Jacob are not consumed."*

Part of this prophecy was fulfilled at the Lord's first coming. The messenger then was John the Baptist. However, most of what was predicted has not yet happened and must therefore find its fulfilment at the end, or after Israel's tribulation. It appears that what has already been fulfilled will be repeated at that time, and the rest of that prophecy will also be fulfilled. The messenger in those future days will be Elijah who together with Moses will appear in Jerusalem, as foretold in Revelation chapter 11. After that preparation has been completed, the Lord will come to his temple, and will do a purifying work amongst his people. Subsequently the leader (the prince; perhaps the resurrected David?) of Israel will present an offering in righteousness. This act may be the eating of bread in the east gate of Jerusalem as described below.

Ezekiel 44:1-3; *"Then he brought me back the way of the gate of the outward sanctuary which looketh toward **the east**; and it [was] shut. Then said the LORD unto me; This gate shall be shut, it shall not be opened, and no man shall enter in by it; because the LORD, the God of Israel, hath entered in by it, therefore it shall be shut. [It is] for the prince; the prince, he shall sit in it to eat bread before the LORD; **he shall enter** by the way of the porch of [that] gate, **and shall go out** by the way of the same."*

Micah 2:12-13; "*I will surely assemble, O Jacob, all of thee; I will surely gather the remnant of Israel; I will put them together as the sheep of Bozrah, as the flock in the midst of their fold: they shall make* **great noise** *by reason of [the multitude of] men. The* **breaker** *is come up* **before** *them*:" (Note: if 'before' refers to time, then this breaking comes before the rest of Jacob is assembled) "*they have broken up, and have passed* **through the gate**, *and are gone out by it: and their king shall pass before them, and the LORD on the head of them.*"

If these two passages above are parallel, then they would describe what will happen after the Lord appeared on the mount of Olives which is east of Jerusalem. The Lord will liberate that city from the mount of Olives. At that time there will come up someone who will break open the east gate of Jerusalem. The Lord will enter Jerusalem through that open gate and go straight to the temple and purify Israel as described above. Now when Israel sees the Lord (whom they have pierced) entering Jerusalem through that gate to go to the temple, a mourning will begin. At that time the Lord will shout from the temple (a voice), to resurrect (refer to the verses below) Israel's Old Testament saints. Their king (David?) thereafter will sit in the east gate, to eat bread (the Lord's supper) before the Lord. This will be regarded as an offering in righteousness.

Matthew 26:30; "*And when they had sung an hymn, they went out into the mount of Olives.*"

After that, a delegation of leading Jews will follow their King who walks in respectful distance behind the Lord. All of them will go out of that east gate, probably back to the mount of Olives (just as 2,000 years before when his disciples followed the Lord to the mount of Olives after the last supper). At the mount the Jews will again (just as his disciples did) witness how the Lord (for the time being) will go back to heaven.

Isaiah 66:6-8; "*A voice of noise from the city, a voice from the temple, a voice of the* **LORD** *that rendereth recompence to his enemies*. *Before she travailed, she brought forth; before her pain came, she was delivered of a man-child. Who hath heard such a thing? Who hath seen such things? Shall the earth be made to bring forth in one day? [or] shall a nation be born at once? for* **as soon as Zion travailed,** *she brought forth her children*."

As soon as Zion travailed she brought forth her children. The word '**travailed**' also means '**pain**' and '**grieved**'. All three words imply internal upheaval, they do not refer to external persecution. As such the passage here cannot refer to the trouble Israel had during that time, but must refer to the painful act of mourning, self-examination and repentance; which will come after they have realised that he whom they have pierced was indeed the very Messiah. When a woman is in travail she is not persecuted from the outside, but suffers from internal pain. But after the birth comes gladness. Likewise, for Israel, after that time of travailing comes joy. The Old Testament saints will come up out of the earth and a new nation will be born. For greater detail about the man-child refer to the chapter '**The Other Man-Child**' in Part Two of this study.

Daniel 12:2; "*And many of them that **sleep in the dust of the earth shall awake**, some to everlasting life, and some to shame [and] everlasting contempt*."

Note: Many will awake, but not all. Probably only the saints of Israel will be resurrected at that time, the wicked will have to wait.

Daniel 12:3; "*And they that be wise shall shine as the brightness of the firmament; and they that turn many to righteousness as the stars for ever and ever*."

They will shine in the same way that Moses did when he came down from mount Sinai.

Ezekiel 37:12-13; "*Therefore prophesy and say unto them, thus saith the Lord GOD; behold, O my people, **I will open your graves, and cause you to come up out of your graves**, and bring you into the land of Israel. And ye shall know that I [am] the LORD, when I have opened your graves, O my people, and brought you up out of your graves*."

Jewish graves of course are to be found all over the world. But all the saved will be raised and brought back to the land of Israel.

Isaiah 26:19 & 21; *"Thy dead [men] shall live, [together with] my dead body shall they arise. Awake and sing, ye that dwell in dust: for thy dew [is as] the dew of herbs, and the earth* **shall cast out the dead**. *... For, behold, the LORD cometh out of his place* **to punish the inhabitants of the earth** *for their iniquity: the earth also shall disclose her blood, and shall no more cover her slain."*

Note that the punishment of the nations follows after the resurrection of the Jewish saints.

Daniel 12:13; *But go thy way till the end [be]: for thou shalt rest, and stand in thy lot at the end of the days."*

Daniel also will be resurrected. After the Lord enters Jerusalem and the temple he will utter his resurrection voice (just as with Lazarus). This will bring forth the saints of the Old Testament. A new nation is born. Now the Lord will pour out upon them the spirit of grace and of supplications, which will melt the stony heart of the Jews. It will be similar to when the Lord breathed on his disciples to equip them for the transition period until Pentecost.

John 20:22; *"And when he had said this, he breathed on [them], and saith unto them, Receive ye the Holy Ghost."*

A great mourning will come over Israel.

Zechariah 12:10-14; *"And I will pour upon the house of David, and upon the inhabitants of Jerusalem, the spirit of grace and of supplications: and they shall look upon me whom they have pierced, and they shall mourn for him, as one mourneth for [his] only [son], and shall be in bitterness for him, as one that is in bitterness for [his] firstborn. In that day shall there be a great mourning in Jerusalem, as the mourning of Hadadrimmon in the valley of Megiddon. And the land shall mourn, every family apart; the family of the house of David apart, and their wives apart; the family of the house of Nathan apart, and their wives apart; the family of the house of Levi apart, and their wives apart; the family of Shimei apart, and their wives apart; All the families that remain, every family apart, and their wives apart."*

First the nations will capture Jerusalem, and ravish the women etc., some time later the leaders of Israel will call out for help from the Lord. The Lord then appears and he will stand on the mount of Olives, which will split in two and therefore provide a safe escape. The Lord will liberate Jerusalem and enter through the east gate. He will go straight to the temple and purify the Jews. Then the Lord will shout, to bring forth the saved of Israel out of the graves of the world. A great mourning of those in Israel follows. The Lord now departs from Jerusalem through the east gate (as described above), to go back to heaven and conduct the fight against Satan and the ungodly from there. Later he will come back to earth with his bride (the Church) for the wedding feast. All this will be necessary to prepare the Jews for the coming kingdom, and to bring the Jews into a state of purity so that Satan no longer has a claim upon them. It will also show them that all of this could have happened 2,000 years ago, had they accepted Christ then and there. All their suffering could have been avoided. The understanding of this, plus the act Christ leaving the Jews again, will probably increase their mourning, and cause some bitterness. But before Christ leaves, he will turn the Jews into invincible fighters, in order that they may defeat the hostile nations around them, and enable the Jews to reclaim their own land.

Zecharaiah 12:6-8; "*In that day will I make the governors of Judah like an hearth of fire among the wood, and like a torch of fire in a sheaf; and they shall devour all the people round about, on the right hand and on the left; and Jerusalem shall be inhabited again in her own place, [even] in Jerusalem. The LORD also shall save the tents of Judah first, that the glory of the house of David and the glory of the inhabitants of Jerusalem do not magnify [themselves] against Judah. In that day shall the LORD defend the inhabitants of Jerusalem; and he that is feeble among them at that day shall be as David; and the house of David [shall be] as God, as the angel of the LORD before them.*"

The Jews will defeat those nations who occupy their land and recover it for themselves. The nations will never again succeed in driving the Jews from their country. Satan, after his forces have been routed, will now gather all the armies of the world into the valley of Jehoshaphat (Joel 3:2 and 3:12), where the Lord himself at his coming as King of kings will destroy them.

What will happen at that time in Jerusalem after the Lord enters through the east gate, could already have come to pass at the Lord's first coming. Take note of the signs in the passage below, and compare them with the previous verses and the one following.

Matthew 27:45 & 50-53; *"Now from the sixth hour there was **darkness** over all the land unto the ninth hour ... Jesus, when he had cried again **with a loud voice**, yielded up the ghost. And, behold, the veil of the temple was rent in twain from the top to the bottom; **and the earth did quake**, and the rocks rent; **And the graves were opened**; and many bodies of the saints which slept arose, And came out of the graves after his resurrection, and went into the holy city, and appeared to many."*

Joel 3:15-16; *"The sun and the moon **shall be darkened**, and the stars shall withdraw their shining. The LORD also **shall roar** out of Zion, and utter his voice from Jerusalem; and the heavens and **the earth shall shake**: but the LORD [will be] the hope of his people, and the strength of the children of Israel."*

Here are similar signs recorded as during the crucifixion. A shout, darkness, and an earthquake. It appears that the crucifixion scene was an indication of what could have happened had Israel repented then and there. The dead could have risen at that time, and Israel's kingdom could have already come. The Joel passage also shows us that at the time when the Lord shall roar out of Zion, Israel's great Tribulation has already terminated. The day of the Lord's wrath has begun, since the signs in the sun and moon are mentioned. Now the day of the Lord breaks upon the nations of the world, darkness and gloominess etc. But Israel will fight in the hope of their soon coming kingdom.

What is the sequence of Israel's gathering?

Zechariah 12:7; *"The LORD also shall save the tents of Judah first, that the glory of the house of David and the glory of the inhabitants of Jerusalem do not magnify [themselves] against Judah."*

First the living of Judah will be saved.

Isaiah 66:7; *"**Before** she travailed, she(*) brought forth; before her*

55

pain came, she was delivered of a man-child."

* The 'she' refers to the earth (refer to the chapter '**The Other Man-Child**' in Part Two). Israel's resurrection occurs before the '**great**' day of the Lord begins, but will come after the time of Jacob's trouble; in other words at the start of the day of the Lord.

Micah 5:3; *"Therefore will he give them up, until the time [that] she which travaileth hath brought forth:* **then the remnant of his brethren shall return unto the children of Israel.**"

The rest of the Jews will be returned later - after 'she' (that is the earth) has brought forth, after the resurrection of the Jewish saints.

Micah 2:12-13; *"I will surely assemble, O Jacob, all of thee, I will surely gather the **remnant** of Israel; I will put them together as the sheep of Bozrah, as the flock in the midst of their fold: they shall make **great noise** by reason of [the multitude of] men."*

Isaiah 27:12-13; *"And it shall come to pass in that day, that the Lord shall beat off from the channel of the river unto the stream of Egypt, and **ye shall be gathered one by one**, O ye children of Israel. And it shall come to pass in that day, that the great **trumpet shall be blown**, and they shall come which were ready to perish in the land of Assyria, and the outcasts in the land of Egypt, and shall worship the Lord in the holy mountain at Jerusalem."*

Some time after the resurrection, the rest of the Jews will also be returned to Israel, which is described in Matthew chapter 24.

Matthew 24:31 & 40-41; *"And he shall send his angels with a **great sound of a trumpet**, and they shall gather together his elect from the four winds, from one end of heaven to the other ... Then shall two be in the field; the one shall be taken, and the other left. Two [women shall be] grinding at the mill; the one shall be taken, and the other left."*

This assembling of the rest of the Jews will take place after the events in Jerusalem have transpired. First all of Judah will be saved. Judah together with the raised saints and the inhabitants of Jerusalem are those which witness first-hand those momentous days as described above. After the Lord has left Jerusalem, but before he returns again with his saints, the rest of the living Jews will be gathered. The angels will gather them from the four winds of the earth, as is recorded in Matthew 24:31 and 24:40-41. That gathering probably takes place just before the Lord returns as King of kings, and that time is unknown. The sequence of events seems to be like this:

1. Israel calls for help, their Tribulation ends, and the day of the Lord starts.

2. The Lord appears on the mount of Olives.

3. Jerusalem is liberated.

4. The Lord enters Jerusalem and the temple, and purifies the Jews.

5. Israel begins to mourn.

6. The Lord shouts from the temple and the Old Testament saints are raised.

7. A new nation is born.

8. The Lord returns to heaven to conduct the fight from there, while Israel liberates most of their land.

9. Satan now gathers the armies of all nations, trying through numbers to overcome invincible Israel. The armies gather in the valley of Jehoshaphat and in Armageddon.

10. The rest of the Jews are gathered into Israel by the angels. The Lord himself comes to destroy those hostile armies.

This seems to be the sequence of events at the time of Jacob's trouble and during the day of the Lord. But how is it possible that, even after all those events have come to pass, and when the Lord returns as King of kings, many Jews are still classified as 'unprofitable servants' and will be sent to hell? There are several explanations for this fact:

1. The absolutely deceitful nature of the human heart. Jeremiah 17:9;

"The heart [is] deceitful above all [things], and desperately wicked: who can know it?" The heart will believe anything, rather than humble itself.

2. During that time there will be spectacular demonstrations of apparently supernatural phenomena. Satan and his host will conduct a great show. That will appeal to the un-converted heart.

3. Miracles alone do not convert a person. When the children of Israel came out of Egypt they witnessed miracles every day, yet the majority of them died as unbelievers in the wilderness.

4. In Luke 16:31, the Lord himself had to say: *"If they hear not Moses and the prophets, neither will they be persuaded, though one rose from the dead."* Also the dead saints are raised during those days - a fact which of itself will not convert the unbeliever's heart. Did the Jews believe after Jesus had raised Lazarus from the dead?

5. In John 21:3 Peter said *"I go a fishing"* ("I go" or " I depart"). In other words he was throwing in the towel to go back to his old life. This he said even after he had already seen the resurrected Lord. Peter was not yet **filled** with the Holy Spirit, he was still acting through his natural mind. Hence those un-converted Jews after Israel's great Tribulation may not all have experienced a true heart conversion, even though they have seen the Lord directly.

All this explains why a significant proportion of the Jews, at that time only made a mental confession for Christ, but their hearts were still un-converted. After the Lord has left them and gone back to heaven, they will soon again be deceived by Satan and his false miracles. They would represent the five foolish virgins, who could not stay alert to wait for the bridegroom, plus those Jews in the world who are left behind by the angels.

Is it possible to identify those two unknown events mentioned in Daniel 12:11-12, those which extend beyond 30 days and 75 days past the end of Israel's tribulation? It could be like this:

The first 30 days are taken up with the liberation and purification of Israel, at the end of which the Lord will go back to heaven.

While the rest of the Jews in the world are admonished to wait until the 75 days have passed, after which time they also will be taken to the land of Israel.

Now we turn to the book of Revelation and analyse how these events outlined so far, join in with those prophecies.

Also for the Greek 'Revelation'

When the Lord Jesus came to this earth for the first time he came to the lost sheep of the nation of Israel, to offer himself as their Messiah. His ministry to the Gentiles was only indirect and secondary. Consequently as was already pointed out, the whole Olivet discourse had to do with the nation of Israel. It was an outline given by Jesus Christ for the future of that nation. But when we come to the book of Revelation things are different. At the very outset of the book of Revelation in chapter 1:1-3 we read that Jesus Christ had given this Revelation to show to his servants, things which must shortly come to pass.

By this time the nation of Israel no longer existed, and the servants to which the Lord referred were Christians. Therefore the book of Revelation addresses primarily the Church and the Gentiles. Israel this time plays only a secondary role. The Olivet discourse was for the Jews. Revelation is primarily for the Gentiles. This follows God's principle, *"to the Jew first, and also to the Greek"* - Roman 1:16. Therefore any event in the book of Revelation should be interpreted as affecting mainly the Gentiles, unless of course the context demands otherwise.

The book of Revelation is often looked upon as a difficult book to comprehend. But once we understand that much of it is written in chronological order, many of the difficulties disappear. For example: The letters to the seven churches from Revelation 2:1 to the end of chapter three are, after an initial address to those actual churches, also an outline of the history of the Church age. Ephesus the first, equals the apostolic church (30 AD to about 100 AD). Followed by Smyrna the martyrs church (100 AD to about 300 AD). Then Pergamum the transition church (300 AD to about 600 AD). After that came the Papal church, represented by Thyatira (600 AD to about 1500 AD). After

59

that Sardis the reformation church (1500 AD to about 1650 AD). Then Philadelphia the missionary church (1650 AD to about 1900 AD). And lastly Laodicea, the ecumenical church (1900 AD to now). Each of these churches occupies a distinct and dominant time in history in chronological order, but of course there are overlaps, and a type of each church can be found today.

Likewise the whole section in Revelation from chapter six to chapter 10 can be interpreted in chronological order if we accept that there is a time gap between the end of the tribulation and the return of the Lord. It is worth noting that whenever John was using the term "**After These Things**", he meant just what he said. That is, John reports one event, and when that one event has ended he reports the next one which follows.

The book of Revelation starts the description of the Tribulation in much the same way as is recorded in the Olivet discourse. The seal judgements describe world war, famine and death, plus the killing of those which testified for God (Revelation 6:4-11). The Olivet discourse describes mainly the events during Israel's Tribulation, because of its relevance to the Jewish nation. On the other hand Revelation which is more concerned with the Gentile nations, records mainly the events which affect those nations. In Revelation we have two references to the 'great tribulation' for the Gentiles. The start of this time cannot be determined, but because 'for the Jew first', it will have to begin later than Israel's Tribulation. There is no reason given in Scripture which compels us to believe that Israel's Tribulation and the Gentile's tribulation have to run parallel. Nor does the length of the Gentile tribulation has to be the same as the one for Israel. They are two independent events. The two references which mention the tribulation for the Gentiles are Revelation 2:22-23 and 7:14.

There is a way in the Bible which allows us to compare Old Testament events or persons with New Testament events or persons. By applying this tool it is possible to gain a better understanding of Scripture. Typology is a good example of this kind of Bible study.

This principle can be expanded by comparing the history of Israel with the history of the Church or Gentile nations. In this way a clue to a particular passage can often be discovered. An example would be the similarity between Israel in the wilderness and the woman of Revelation chapter 12 in the wilderness. This similarity is shown and explained in Part Two of this study. There is also another example of similarities between two Scriptures. If we compare the early visions of Ezekiel with John's vision at the throne of God and the passage concerning the angel who stands on the sea and the earth, we discover a similar set of circumstances. This allows us to draw conclusions regarding the purpose of both Scripture sections. **Chart No 2** on Page 62 sets out some of the similarities between the two visions.

When Ezekiel received his first vision, he was a captive who was taken to the land of the Chaldeans. The time was about 595 BC. Jerusalem had already been captured once, yet Judah still existed as a kingdom. God's wrath was upon Judah. It was a time of transition. The kingdom of Judah was in decline, the time of the Gentiles was emerging. God continued to warn his people, but to no avail. As a result God judged the Jews, their kingdom came to an end, and the 'Times of the Gentiles' began.

In the book of Revelation beginning at chapter four, until chapter 10, a reversal of history takes place. Chapters four and five describe the Tribulation and other events. The Gentiles are still in control of Jerusalem, but the wrath of God already affects the Gentile nations. It is again, as formerly in the days of Ezekiel, a time of transition. But this time it is the other way around. The time of the Gentiles is drawing to a rapid close, and Israel's coming kingdom knocks at the door. From chapter six to chapter ten, the day of the Lord's wrath is described in chronological order. From now on God's full wrath is directed against the unrepentant Gentiles.

There Ezekiel's visions marked the end of Judah's kingdom and the start of the Times of the Gentiles. But now in Revelation John's visions reverses the order. They mark the end of the times of the Gentiles and foreshadow the soon coming kingdom of Israel.

The eating of the books by the two prophets, Ezekiel 3:1-3, and Revelation 10:9, would therefore, in each instance, signify the termination of an era.

Chart No 2 - on the following page - shows that the circumstances and setting of Ezekiel's and John's visions are similar.

Chart No 2 - Similarities between Ezekiel's and John's Visions

Ezekiel	Revelation
Four living creatures; faces like a man, lion, ox and eagle. 1:10	Four creatures; appearance like a lion, calf and eagle, face like a man. 4:7
Ezekiel saw the Lord on a throne. 1:26 & 28	John saw the Lord on a throne. 4:3 & 10
Ezekiel saw a rainbow round about the throne. 1:26 & 28	John saw a rainbow round about the throne. 4:3
The Lord on a throne, his upper and lower body (feet), had the appearance of fire and brightness, a rainbow round about. 1:27-28	Christ's feet like burning brass, countenance like the sun, 1:15-16. The angel (Christ) had a rainbow upon his head, face like the sun, feet like pillars of fire. 10:1
Ezekiel was sent down to warn Israel. 3:17	Revelation is a warning to the Gentiles of God's coming wrath.
Ezekiel had to eat a book (or scroll). 3:1-3	John had to eat a book or scroll. 10:9
The scroll had writings on the front and back. 2:10	The scroll had writings on the front and back. 5:1
Book was full of lamentations, mourning and woe. 2:10	Book contains the 7 seal judgments which are full of wrath and woe. 6:1 & 17, plus 8:1-2 & 13
Book tasted sweet to Ezekiel, but caused bitterness. 3:3 & 3:14	Book was sweet in John's mouth, but bitter in his belly. 10:10
Ezekiel was taken up by the Spirit. 3:12-14	John was taken up to heaven in his spirit. 4:2
Despite all warnings in the days of Ezekiel, Israel never repented, and suffered wrath.	During the day of the Lord the Gentiles will not repent, they will suffer wrath. 9:21

The Lamb's Wrath upon the Nations

Revelation 6:12-14 & 17; *"And I beheld when he had opened the sixth seal, and, lo, there was a great earthquake; and the sun became black as sackcloth of hair, and the moon became as blood; And the stars of heaven fell unto the earth, even as a fig tree casteth her untimely figs, when she is shaken of a mighty wind. And the heaven departed as a scroll when it is rolled together; and every mountain and island were moved out of their places.... for the great day of wrath is come; and who shall be able to stand?"*

The same signs in Matthew 24 and Luke 21 herald the same point in time, the end of Israel's Tribulation. But here some additional events are recorded, like the moving of every island and mountain. The ungodly of the earth recognise this as the beginning of '**The Great Day of the Lamb's Wrath**'. They are terrified but do not repent of their sins. Nor do they understand the significance of this time since God has sent them strong delusions.

The sealing of the 144,000 Jews is the next event. Please observe that this happens after the time of Jacob's trouble when God no longer judges Israel. According to 2 Corinthians 3:16, the veil of blindness covers the heart of Israel because of unbelief, but when they turn to the Lord, the veil will be removed and they will understand. Likewise in Romans 11:23 Paul states that if Israel turns from unbelief they will be grafted back into the olive tree from which they are broken off. Therefore as long as Israel rejects the Lord Jesus Christ, they are smitten with blindness and remain as broken off branches. However, after the time of Jacob's trouble things have changed. By this time many have repented and can now be used by God.

Now there arises the question ... "What is the purpose of the sealing of these 144,000 Jews? Well, obviously to protect them in order that they will survive that time. However, is there a way by which we can discover the function of these Jews? There may be - the clue would be their number, twelve thousand of each tribe.

Revelation 7:5; *"Of the tribe of Juda [were] sealed twelve thousand. Of the tribe of Reuben [were] sealed twelve thousand. Of the tribe of*

Gad [were] sealed twelve thousand."

In the Old Testament whenever a group of twelve thousand servants are mentioned (as here in Revelation), they are always seen to be in active military service (compare with Judges 21:10; 2 Samuel 10:6 & 17:1; 1 Kings 4:26 & 10:26; 2 Chronicles 1:14 and 9:25).

Therefore perchance, these 12 times 12,000 Jewish servants here are also engaged in military service after Israel's Tribulation, that is during the day of the Lord. Perhaps they are sealed to become those invincible fighters as mentioned in Zechariah 12:6-8. But this is only speculation and by no means certain.

Revelation Chapter Seven

Revelation 7:9-10; *"After this I beheld, and, lo, a great multitude, which no man could number, of all nations, and kindreds, and people, and tongues, stood before the throne, and before the lamb, clothed with white robes, and **palms** in their hands; And cried with a loud voice, saying, Salvation to our God which sitteth upon the throne, and unto the lamb."*

Now the spotlight is turned on to a group of people out of every nation which came out of great tribulation. These saints came to repentance during the great tribulation for the Gentiles. As will be shown later, many events in the Bible occur twice. Israel experienced a 'day of God's wrath' during the time of the Babylonian captivity (Zephaniah 1:14-18). The Gentiles likewise will experience such a day as has been shown. Again Israel will suffer 'great tribulation' (which is the time of Jacob's trouble), as recorded in the Olivet discourse. The Gentiles also will suffer great tribulation in order that the chosen ones will repent and come to Christ. The purpose for tribulation is never wrath, but to lead God's people to repentance. The saints mentioned above must be Gentiles who never repented before the rapture. The fact that these saints carry palm branches could be a clue to who they are. Palm branches were carried by the Jews at the feast of tabernacles (Leviticus 23:40-42). That feast was to be a memorial for their wilderness wanderings (Leviticus 23:43). Therefore the palms in the hands of these saints may indicate that they came out of the wilderness, which would identify them as the remnant of the woman's seed

(Revelation 12). As will be shown, those who are part of the remnant of the woman will be killed in the wilderness.

Revelation 2:18-23; "*And unto the angel of the church in Thyatira write; These things saith the Son of God, who hath his eyes like unto a flame of fire, and his feet [are] like fine brass; I know **thy works, and charity**, and service, and faith, and thy patience, and thy works; and the last [to be] more than the first. Notwithstanding I have a few things against thee, because thou sufferest that woman Jezebel, which calleth herself a prophetess, to teach and to seduce my servants to commit fornication, and to eat things sacrificed unto idols. And I gave her space to repent of her fornication; and she repented not. Behold, I will cast her into a bed, and them that commit adultery with her into **great tribulation**, except they repent of their deeds. And I will **kill her children** with death; and all the churches shall know that I am he which searcheth the reins and hearts: and I will give unto every one of you **according to your works**.*"

As will be shown later, the woman of Revelation chapter 12 represents the visible Church as seen by the world. This visible Church includes saved and unsaved people. The saved will be removed from the earth by the rapture, but the professing Christians will be left behind. They represent the remnant of the woman's seed, many of them will, during the time when Satan persecutes them, come in true repentance to the foot of the cross. As shall be shown, the visible Church includes Roman Catholicism and apostate Protestantism. It was already pointed out that the church of **Thyatira** (Revelation 2:18-23), could very well represent the papal Church. If that is so, then her children which will be killed in great tribulation could represent part of the remnant of the woman's seed. These Christians, plus many others out of all nations will, during the time of the Gentile tribulation, come in true repentance to Christ. They would be martyred for their faith and would therefore go to heaven. They would indeed be coming out of great tribulation, as is stated in verses 13-15. May we never forget that God is gracious; he observes the many works of charity which multitudes of Roman Catholics perform, believing they will save them. Of course, these works cannot save anyone, yet God will remember, and prove those who have done them. They will be tested during that tribulation under totally new circumstances. If they love Christ more than their own life, and are prepared to die for their faith, they will be saved. Obviously multitudes do, they would be those tribulation saints mentioned in these verses.

Revelation 7:13-15; *"And one of the elders answered, saying unto me, What are these which are arrayed in white robes? and whence came they? And I said unto him, Sir, thou knowest. And he said to me, These are they which came out of great tribulation, and have washed their robes, and made them white in the blood of the Lamb. Therefore are they before the throne of God, and serve him day and night **in his temple**: and he that sitteth on the throne shall dwell among them."*

These Tribulation saints (perhaps the remnant of the woman's seed, see Part Two for detail) are dedicated to serve God in his heavenly temple. They will never go down to earth, since the sun will not shine on them any more. They are the equivalent of Israel's Levites who served God in his temple on earth.

Revelation 7:16; *"They shall hunger no more, neither thirst any more; neither shall the sun light on them, nor any heat."*

The mentioning about hunger, thirst, sun and heat would also indicate that these Gentile tribulation saints came out of the wilderness, which again may point to the fact that they might be the remnant of the woman of Revelation chapter 12, who had to flee into a wilderness.

The elder who asked John a question and then answered it himself, must be one of the 24 elders mentioned in Revelation 4:4. That these elders represent the Church seems to be indicated in Revelation 5:10, where they explain that God had made them kings and priests. This office will be held by Christians as is revealed in Peter's epistle:

1 Peter 2:9; *"But ye are a chosen generation, a royal priesthood."*

That this group of tribulation saints mentioned above form a separate group, and do not belong to the Church is also hinted at by the way the elder formulates his question and answer. He talks about them as a different group, apart from himself. Likewise John, if these tribulation saints were part of the Church, should have known since he himself is part of the Church.

Revelation Chapter Eight

Revelation 8:1-2; *"And when he had opened the seventh seal, there was silence in heaven for about the space of half an hour. And I saw the seven angels which stood before God; and to them were given seven trumpets."*

Chapter eight starts with the opening of the last seal. This action introduces the seven trumpet judgements. The time of these trumpet blasts starts after the Tribulation and terminates before the second coming of the Lord. The trumpets are blown in succession and each starts one specific judgement, except the last trumpet. These judgements are directed against the nations of the world. Since the main purpose of Part One of this study is to outline the order of the last day events, most of the details of these judgements will be omitted.

The first four trumpets start judgements which affect one third of the earth, the oceans, the rivers and the stars. The duration of these events could be over in a few days or weeks. After the fourth trumpet, an angel pronounces three woes. These woes indicate that the last three trumpets are especially severe. They follow in succession, one after the other. Inside the section which describes the trumpet judgements, there are some other events recorded which are not part of those judgements. Each of the three woes is the direct result of an angel blowing his trumpet. Trumpet five triggers the first woe, trumpet six the second woe, and trumpet seven the third woe.

Revelation Chapter Nine

Revelation 9:3-4; *"And there came out of the smoke locusts upon the earth: and unto them was given power, as the scorpions of the earth have power.... And it was commanded them that they should not hurt the grass of the earth, neither any green thing, neither any tree; but only those men which have not the seal of God in their foreheads."*

The fifth trumpet judgement releases the locusts out of the bottomless pit, this is the first woe. No specific geographical extent of this plague is given and since it is directed against the wicked of the world, we have no compelling reason to assume that Israel will be affected by those locusts.

After the Tribulation the wrath of the Lamb is directed primarily against the world, and Israel is affected indirectly, or not at all. However, the 144,000 Jewish servants are on earth, and need to be protected. Therefore the locusts are not permitted to harm those Jews in the world who have God's seal on their forehead. One interesting point is recorded in Revelation 9:10. Those locusts are said to have power to hurt men for five months. Could this be the minimum duration of the time interval between the end of the Tribulation and the coming of the Lord?

Revelation 9:13-14; *"And the sixth angel sounded, and I heard a voice from the four horns of the golden altar which is before God. Saying to the sixth angel which had the trumpet, loose the four angels which are bound in the great river Euphrates."*

The sixth trumpet announces the loosening of four demonic spirits who will control an army of 200 million and together kill one third of mankind. Now note that while God's judgement on Israel turned the Jews in repentance to Jesus Christ, the wicked Gentiles under judgement refuse to repent as is stated in verses 20 & 21.

The loosening of the four fallen angels is the result of the sixth trumpet blast and starts the second woe. This woe continues through much of the Day of the Lord, but terminates some time before the second coming of the Lord with his saints. John's account from heaven is now interrupted, because in chapter 10 he finds himself on earth. Therefore he is not able to continue to report the termination of the second woe, until he re-enters the heavenly scene in chapter 11.

Revelation Chapter 10

Revelation 10:1-2; *"And I saw another mighty angel **come down** from heaven, clothed with a cloud: and a rainbow was upon his head, and his face was as it were the sun, and his feet as pillars of fire: And he had in his hand a little book open, and he set his right foot upon the sea, and his left foot on the earth."*

John now observes an angel coming down from heaven, to rest his feet on the sea and the earth. This means that this is an earthly scene and that John himself must have left heaven and is back on earth. The description of this seems to indicate that this may be the Lord Jesus claiming legal possession of the earth. This event happens during the time of the second woe, but is not actually a part of that woe. The woe itself consists only in the loosing of the four fallen angels and the result of that action.

Revelation 10:6-7; *"And sware by him that liveth for ever and ever, who created heaven, and the things that therein are, and the earth, and the things that therein are, and the sea, and the things which are therein, that there should be time no longer: But in the days of the voice of the seventh angel, when he shall begin to sound, the mystery of God should be finished, as he hath declared to his servants the prophets."*

The angel declares that the end of the time interval has come, and that after the seventh angel begins to sound the mystery programme of God will be finished, as was declared by the prophets. In other words, when the seventh angel begins to sound, Jesus Christ will take over the kingdoms of the world. Then the third woe, which incorporates the seven vials will begin, and he will reveal himself to the world by coming in glory to set up his eternal kingdom. John is told to go to the angel and to take his book, and the angel tells him to eat it. In order to comply with that request, John himself obviously has to be on earth. As has been previously pointed out, the eating of that book heralds the termination of the times of the Gentiles.

Revelation 10:11; *"And he said unto me, Thou must prophesy again before many peoples, and nations, and tongues, and kings."*

This now brings us to the end of John's first chronological outline of his visions. Until now everything was in order and sequence. At this point he is told to start again to prophesy. From now on, until the end of the book of Revelation, John will retrace the ground already covered and fill in details which he had left out before. He will also go further by showing the end of God's redemptive programme. This retracing of events already described is not new. In Genesis, the first book of the Bible, the same method is used. There God gave a general outline of the creation in chapter one, then in chapter two from verse four to the end of the chapter he gave a second different outline of the creation account. Here in the last book of the Bible this method is repeated. John will continue to change his place of observation, he will report from heaven or from earth. This point has to be kept in mind, since this fact influences the interpretation of his visions.

Revelation Chapter 11

John now continues his account from an earthly perspective. The first chronological outline has finished and from now on he fills in details which he could not report in the previous sequence of events. The context and duration of these events indicate that they must start during the time of the Tribulation. The measuring of the temple, and the Gentile dominion over it, probably run concurrently with the 3½ years of the time of Jacob's trouble. In Malachi 4:5-6, we are informed that Elijah will come before the Day of the Lord, and as has already been shown, Elijah must be one of those two witnesses. Therefore the start of their ministry has to be inside the time of Israel's Tribulation. The witnesses will prophesy inside Jerusalem against the world. Their ministry concerns the Jews and the Gentiles. Those witnesses will be overcome after 3½ years by the Antichrist, who must therefore at that time still be in control of Jerusalem. This fact would indicate that Antichrist's victory over them would have to be at the end of Israel's Tribulation. Because after Israel has repented the Lord will come and fight for them, the Jews will be turned into invincible fighters and Antichrist and all his hordes will be thrown out of Jerusalem.

Zechariah 12:8; *"In that day shall the LORD defend the inhabitants of Jerusalem; and he that is feeble among them at that day shall be as David; and the house of David [shall be] as God, as the angel of the LORD before them."*

Zechariah 14:13-14; *"And it shall come to pass in that day, [that] a great tumult from the LORD shall be among them; and they shall lay hold every one on the hand of his neighbour, and his hand shall rise up against the hand of his neighbour. And Judah also shall fight at Jerusalem; and the wealth of all the heathen round about shall be gathered together, gold, and silver, and apparel, in great abundance."*

After reporting the events in Jerusalem at the end of Israel's Tribulation, John again enters the heavenly scene. The first thing he hears there is the proclamation that the second woe has finished, but that the third woe will follow immediately. It almost looks as if heaven has been waiting for him to return, in order to continue with the programme. The seventh trumpet, according to Revelation 8:13, starts the third woe. The sounding of the last trumpet by the seventh angel ushers in the end phase of the day of the Lord. The kingdoms of the world will now be taken over by the Lord himself. Then in verse 19 a brief outline of the third woe is given . This woe includes the seven vial judgments of chapters 15 and 16. This means that the seventh trumpet which introduces the third woe includes the seven vials, just as the seventh seal included the seven trumpets.

Now we compare the two parallel passages of Isaiah chapter 24 and Revelation chapter 12, plus the principle of the double occurrence in the Bible.

Chart No 3 - Table of Double Occurrences

Description	1st Occurrence	Scripture	2nd Occurrence	Scripture
World wide judgments	The flood	Gen 6:7	Day of the Lord	Isa 2:12
	One for the Jews	Zep 1:14-18	One for the Gentiles	Oba 1:15
Day of the Lord	One for Israel	Mat Ch 24	One for the Gentiles	Rev 2:22
Great Tribulations	Through the Red Sea	Ex 14:22	Through Jordan	Jos 3:13
Crossings through	The old covenant	Heb 8:13	The new covenant	Heb 8:13
water	One on earth	Gen 6:18	One in heaven	Rev 11:19
Covenants	One for the earth	Lk 11:2	One in heaven	Jn 18:36
Arks of God	Judah	2 Ch 11:17	Israel	1 Ki 21:7
Kingdoms of God	The old - in Israel	----	The new - from Heaven	Rev 3:12
Jewish Kingdoms	One literal - in Iraq	Gen 10:10	One symbolic - Rome	Rev Ch 17
Jerusalems	The Jews	----	The Gentiles	----
Babylons	The present	----	The future	Isa 65:17
Peoples	Judgment seat of Christ	Rom 14:10	Great White Throne	Rev 20:11
Worlds	One in heaven	Rev 14:13	One in hell	Mat 18:9
Judgment Seats	First - natural	----	Second - spiritual	Jn 3:3
Destinies	First - natural	Heb 9:27	Second - spiritual	Rev 21:8
Types of birth	First - of the earth	1 Cor 15:45	Second - from above	1 Cor 15:45
Types of death	Israel - wife of the Father	Isa 54:5-6	Church - wife of Christ	2 Cor 11:2
Adams	12 from Israel?	Rev 4:4	12 from the Church?	Rev 4:4
Wives		Rev 13:4	False Prophet	Rev 13:11
Groups of elders			As a King	
Beasts				

Events in that Day

There seems to be a principle in the Bible by which events repeat themselves, or certain things occur twice. If this can be taken as a general rule, then some passages can obtain a new meaning, or become easier to understand. For example, the prophecy about Babylon in Revelation chapters 17 and 18 will become clearer if this principle is applied. Likewise, the apparent discrepancies with regard to the 144,000, as recorded in chapters seven and 14, will disappear if it is accepted that there are two groups of 144,000 saints. One group consists of Jews, the other of Gentiles. **Refer to Chart No 3** on the previous page, which lists many such double occurrences as found in the Bible.

We will now apply this principle to the two above-mentioned examples and see if they do fit in with Scripture. If the 24th chapter of Isaiah is read in conjunction with the 14th of Revelation, then a broad outline of the 'day of the Lord' can be discovered.

Revelation 14:1-5; *"And I looked, and, lo, a Lamb stood on the mount Zion, and with him an hundred forty [and] four thousand, having his Father's name written in their foreheads. And I heard a voice from heaven, as the voice of **many waters**, and as the voice of a great thunder: and I heard the voice of harpers harping with their harps: And they sung as it were a new song before the throne, and before the four beasts, and the elders: and no man could learn that song but the hundred [and] forty [and] four thousand, which were redeemed **from the earth**. These are they which were not defiled with women; for they are virgins These are they which follow the Lamb whithersoever he goeth. These were redeemed from **among men**, [being] the first fruits unto God and to the Lamb. And in their mouth was found no guile: for they are without fault before the throne of God."*

Here it is stated that 144,000 virgins stood with the Lord Jesus on mount Zion. Who are these saints? Are they identical with the 144,000 Jewish servants of chapter seven? Or is it possible that these 144,000 virgins are the Gentile counterpart of the 144,000 Jews mentioned in chapter seven? The fact that these virgins stand on mount Zion does not prove that they are Jews, since it is explicitly stated that they follow the Lord wherever he goes. Consequently they don't have to have any connection with mount Zion or any other city.

Can the 'double principle' be applied in this case? It would seem so. Every Christian who holds the pre-tribulation position would agree that the 144,000 sealed servants of chapter seven are Jews. But why are these 144,000 virgins of chapter 14 said to be the redeemed from the earth? This does not sound Jewish. Furthermore, they were in heaven before the throne of God. Which means they must have already died and been in heaven before they appeared on mount Zion. They had been singing whilst in heaven, and their voice was as the voice of many nations (waters). This indicates that they are saved Gentiles. The Jews of chapter seven are sealed, presumably for protection, which implies that they will be destined to survive the day of the Lord on earth, they don't have to die. This fact that the saints of Israel will all survive the time of their Tribulation is written in Daniel 12:1, and if they live through that time on earth, then they cannot be in heaven.

These 144,000 of chapter fourteen are virgins, who are not defiled with woman. What does that mean? Is every man who has a woman defiled? If that is the meaning, then every Christian who has a wife would have to be considered as defiled with her. But in Hebrews 13:4 we read "The marriage bed is undefiled." Also, the question has to be asked, "Are there no female saints in this group?" Clearly then, the term virgins here has to be understood in a spiritual context. Since it is stated that 'woman would defile a person' those women mentioned here cannot represent literal woman. Scripture, in a symbolical sense, speaks of two kinds of woman:

1.   The virtuous, like the bride of the Lamb.

2.   The defiled, like the mother and her harlot daughters of Revelation 17.

A woman therefore can depict a body of religious people. An assembly of true Christians would represent a virtuous woman (compare with 2 John verses 1 and 13). On the other hand, an assembly of apostates or heretics would characterise a harlot, and a person going into such a woman (assembly) would be defiled. Such a person would be seen to have spiritual intercourse with a harlot, and would no longer be innocent, it could not be said that such a man or woman was a virgin. These 144,000 of Revelation chapter 14 therefore are persons who never belonged to any church, neither true or apostate. If they had belonged to a true church and were saved, they would have been removed by the rapture. But if they had belonged to an apostate church they would have lost their virginity. These must be persons who never heard the true gospel, they would be those who came from countries where the Christian gospel was suppressed. These virgins are said to be the firstfruits. This gives us a clue to understanding who they are.

The context of the first part of chapter 14 indicates that the events described here occur before the day of the Lord during the Tribulation. In verses 14 to 16 we are informed that the Son of man brings in his harvest. He reaps those which are his from the earth. It follows that the 144,000 virgins represent the firstfruits of the end time. They are those who have never belonged to any church and are most likely those who came from countries where the Christian gospel could not be freely preached. They do not belong to the remnant of the woman of Revelation 12, because the remnant consists of formerly nominal Christians who all belonged to a Christian denomination. The others who are reaped subsequently by the Son of man (Revelation 14:14-16), are saved later and would have a similar background as these virgins. The virgins are the firstfruits, the others make up the main harvest of the end time.

There is an interesting scenario: Could it be that the 144,000 virgins of chapter 14 are the companions of the king's daughter, as described in Psalm 45? (Refer to the chapter '**The Church in Psalm 45**').

In verse one of Revelation 14, John saw the Lamb with the 144,000 virgins, stand on mount Zion. It should be pointed out that this is not the same event as described in Zechariah 14:1-4. In the latter passage it is written that the Lord will stand on the mount of Olives, not on mount Zion. The appearing of the Lord on the mount of Olives will happen just after the end of Israel's Tribulation, when he will help them. But the appearing of the Lord on mount Zion must take place after his return as King to judge the nations (Matthew 25:31-46). Those 144,000 virgins would have come back from heaven with the Lord, since it is stated that they *follow the Lamb whithersoever he goeth.*"

Angels Preach

Revelation 14:6-7; *"And I saw another angel fly in the midst of heaven, having the everlasting gospel to preach unto them that dwell on the earth, and to every nation, and kindred, and tongue, and people, Saying with a loud voice, Fear God, and give glory to him; for **the hour of his judgment** is come: and worship him that made heaven, and earth, and the sea, and the fountains of waters."*

The next event revealed in Revelation 14 is the preaching of the gospel to all nations by an angel. The word heaven here must have reference to the sky. Satan and Antichrist by that time have closed every avenue for people to hear the gospel. He probably thinks that he now has the world for himself. But God is never defeated, and he sends one of his angels to do what men can no longer do. God has the appropriate answer for every situation. That this preaching has the desired effect can be seen later in verses 14 to 16 of that chapter, where the Lord reaps the earth of its harvest of saved people. We can also find out more about the effects of this preaching, when we turn to Isaiah 24, which is the parallel passage to Revelation 14. In verses 14 and 15 of Isaiah 24, we read about those from the isles of the sea (Gentile people) who sing and give glory to the Lord. This is what the angel in Revelation 14, while preaching, had asked the Gentile nation to do; *"give glory to God"*. His preaching in association with the judgments as described in Isaiah 24, would have led many of the heathen to repentance. How many people who today seek for signs and wonders, may say, "if I only saw a miracle, then I would believe". In those days they will see a miracle, they will see and hear angels preaching, many will believe, but the others will be left with no excuse. The angel also proclaimed that the hour of judgment had come. This also fits the context of Isaiah 24. But let's start from verse one of Isaiah 24. This announcement by the angel that the hour of judgment has come, explains why the wicked, as recorded in Revelation 6:17, know that *"the Lamb's great day of wrath"* has come. They know because the angel, while preaching in the sky, told them. Therefore the events of Revelation 6:12-17, which usher in the day of the Lord, must start soon after the preaching of the angel.

Isaiah 24:1-3; *"Behold, the LORD maketh the earth empty, and maketh it waste, and turneth it upside down, and scattereth abroad the inhabitants thereof. And it shall be, as with the people, so with the priest; as with the servant, so with his master; as with the maid, so with her mistress; as with the buyer, so with the seller; as with the lender, so with the borrower; as with the taker of usury, so with the giver of usury to him. The land shall be utterly emptied, and utterly spoiled: for the LORD hath spoken this word."*

The coming judgment against the whole earth is proclaimed, and a general overview is given. The earth shall be depopulated. There will be no difference between the people, every sinner, without distinction, will be judged.

Isaiah 24:4-6. *"The earth mourneth [and] fadeth away, the world languisheth [and] fadeth away, the haughty people of the earth do languish. The earth also is **defiled under the inhabitants** thereof; because they have transgressed the laws, changed the ordinance, broken the everlasting covenant. Therefore hath the curse devoured the earth, and they that dwell therein are desolate: therefore the inhabitants of the earth are burned, and few men left."*

The day of the Lord comes upon the people of the world because of their wickedness. Few will survive that time. The term 'few' has to be seen to be relative to today's massive world population. It has been estimated that perhaps only about 50-million people throughout the whole world may survive.

The City of Confusion

Isaiah 24:7-12; *"The new wine mourneth, the vine languisheth, all the merryhearted do sigh. The mirth of tabrets ceaseth, the noise of them that rejoice endeth, the joy of the harp ceaseth. They shall not drink wine with a song; strong drink shall be bitter to them that drink it. The city of confusion is broken down; every house is shut up, that no man may come in. [There is] a crying for wine in the streets; all joy is darkened, the mirth of the land is gone. In the city is left desolation, and the gate is smitten with destruction."*

Now the inspired text focuses on some of the details of that time. The general conditions in the world are described, but specifically those of a city. The city is called the city of confusion. There is a city in the Bible with a name which means confusion - it is Babylon. This city is described in the Old Testament and in Revelation chapters 17 and 18.

But just as there are two Jerusalems, likewise there are two Babylon's. One is called Mystery Babylon, which is generally understood to be Rome. The other is the literal city of Babylon in modern Iraq.

This fact about the two Babylons has caused a little puzzlement. Some Christians connect Rome with every prophecy in Revelation where Babylon is mentioned, while others insist that literal Babylon will have to be rebuilt, in order to fulfil every prophecy which was made about that city. The scope of this study does not allow us to investigate in detail those positions. Just that much, indeed some prophecies in connection with literal Babylon still need to be fulfilled and therefore the city will have to be rebuilt in order to complete prophecy. It would appear then that Revelation 17 describes Mystery Babylon which must be Rome, while Revelation 18 describes the destruction of a new, yet to be rebuilt, Babylon. The context of Isaiah 24 seems to indicate that the city of confusion mentioned in that chapter refers to Rome, rather than to literal Babylon, for the following reasons:

1. It is stated that there is a general lamenting about the fact that the wine has been cut off. Literal Babylon is situated in a Muslim country, they don't drink wine or alcohol. They certainly would not openly complain in the streets if alcohol was not available.

2. Rome has a population which is known to enjoy song and wine, therefore the description *"they shall not drink [any more] wine with a song"* would fit the customs of that city.

3. The term 'city of confusion' means 'Babylon' the name mentioned in Revelation 17, which is generally understood to be Rome.

4. The destruction of the Gate (or gates) is mentioned in verse 12. Rome has some famous Gates, the Gate of 'Septimus-Severus', 'The Arc of Titus' and the 'Arc of Constantine' for example.

Isaiah 24:13-16; " *When thus it shall be in the midst of the land among the people, [there shall be] as the shaking of an olive tree, [and] as the gleaning grapes when the vintage is done. They shall lift up their voice, they shall sing for the majesty of the LORD, they shall cry aloud from the sea, Wherefore glorify ye the LORD in the fires, [even] the name of the LORD God of Israel in the isles of the sea. From the uttermost part of the earth have we heard songs, [even] glory to the righteous. But I said, My leanness, my leanness, woe unto me! the treacherous dealers have dealt treacherously; yea, the treacherous dealers have dealt very treacherously."*

5. The next event mentioned in Isaiah 24 is the gleaning of people from the earth. Those which are gleaned are those saved in response to the preaching of the angel as mentioned in Revelation 14, they give glory to the Lord. These events probably take place during the great tribulation for the Gentiles. Therefore first the city is destroyed, then people rejoice in the Lord. This is the same sequence of events as mentioned in Revelation 14, where it is stated that "*Babylon* (Rome?) *is fallen is fallen*".

Revelation 14:8; "*And there followed another angel, saying, Babylon is fallen, is fallen, that great city, because she made all nations drink of the wine of the wrath of her fornication.*"

After the preaching of the everlasting gospel, another angel proclaims that Babylon is fallen, is fallen, which means it **has already fallen**. It fell before the angel preached the gospel. Therefore the same sequence of events is recorded; both prophets refer to the same city in both passages.

These five points above could favour the view that the city of Isaiah 24 refers to Rome, that is mystery Babylon. However one can't be sure and it is still possible that indeed literal, yet to be rebuilt city of Babylon, could be in view in these verses.

The Treacherous Dealers

Now the prophet Isaiah continues with his description of the end time. After reporting the songs of the righteous from the uttermost part of the earth, the prophet utters a strange sentence.

Isaiah 24:16; "*From the uttermost part of the earth have we heard songs, [even] glory to the righteous. But I said, my leanness, my leanness, woe unto me!* **the treacherous dealers have dealt treacherously; ye, the treacherous dealers have dealt very treacherously**."

After reporting the songs of the righteous, Isaiah laments about treacherous dealers. In order to understand what he means, we must read this verse in conjunction with Revelation 14. There, in verse seven, we read about the angel preaching the everlasting gospel. The result of that preaching according to Isaiah 24, is the breaking forth of the joyful songs in the uttermost parts of the earth. But after the preaching of the gospel another angel warns about the mark of the beast. This would indicate that the revival which had taken place because of the angel's preaching is soon restrained by the treacherous servants of Satan and Antichrist. The treacherous act they perform is probably the forcing of the '**mark of the beast**' upon the people of the world. This would certainly stifle any revival. Therefore the prophet laments about these treacherous dealers. God responds to this treachery with a warning uttered by an angel.

Revelation 14:9-11; "*And the third angel followed them, saying with a loud voice, If any man worship the beast and his image, **and receive [his] mark** in his forehead, or in his hand, The same shall drink of the wine of the wrath of God, which is poured out without mixture into the cup of his indignation; and he shall be tormented with fire and brimstone in the presence of the holy angels, and in the presence of the Lamb: And the smoke of their torment ascendeth up for ever and ever: and they have no rest day nor night, who worship the beast and his image, and whosoever receiveth the mark of his name*."

The angel warns of the serious consequences for anybody taking the mark of the beast. Therefore all the people of those days have heard the preaching of the gospel, and have been warned by an angel not to take Satan's mark. If, in spite of all this, they still accept the mark, they will have no excuse.

Revelation 14:12-13; *"Here is the patience of the saints: here [are] they that keep the commandments of God, and the faith of Jesus. And I heard a voice from heaven saying unto me, Write, blessed [are] the dead which die in the Lord from henceforth: Yea, saith the Spirit, that they may rest from their labours; and their works do follow them."*

The righteous are exhorted to stay firm, not to give in to the treachery of the satanic forces, not to accept the mark. The promise is given, that if they keep the commandments of God and have faith in Jesus, then from now on if they die in Christ, they would go straight to heaven and their works will be rewarded to them.

Revelation 14:14-16; *"And I looked, and behold, a white cloud, and upon the cloud [one] sat like unto the Son of man, having on his head a golden crown, and in his hand a sharp sickle. And another angel came out of the temple, crying with a loud voice to him that sat on the cloud, Thrust in thy sickle, and reap: for the time is come for thee to reap; for the harvest of the earth is ripe. And he that sat on the cloud thrust in his sickle on the earth; and the earth was reaped."*

John 4:35; *"Say not ye, There are yet four month and [then] cometh harvest? Behold, I say unto you, lift up your eyes, and look on the fields; for they are white already unto harvest."*

As was already mentioned, the Lord himself reaps his harvest from the earth. After this the Gentile tribulation probably finishes, since those who would repent by now have repented. The last saints are taken home. It appears that from this point forward there will proceed only judgment from heaven. The time of grace for the world seems to have past, the day of the Lord's wrath breaks upon the wicked. However, there must be other Gentiles who also reject the mark of Antichrist, but will not die, and they represent the sheep of Matthew 25. This group of saints mentioned above, who are reaped by Christ himself and are taken to heaven, are referred to in the 15th chapter of Revelation.

Revelation 15:2-3; (Weymouth New Testament 1912) *"And I saw what seemed to be a sea of glass mingled with fire, and those who had gained the victory over the Wild Beast and over his statue and the number of his name, standing by the sea of glass and having harps which belonged to God. And they were singing the song of Moses, God's servant, and the song of the Lamb. Their words were "Great and wonderful are Thy works, O Lord God, the Ruler of all. Righteous and true are Thy ways, O King of the nations."*

As was already pointed out before, there will be no Jews amongst the tribulation saints which are in heaven, since every elect Jew will survive that time on earth. It is often said that these saints in the above verses must be Jews, because they sing the song of Moses. But this does not have to be so, because the song of Moses in Deuteronomy chapter 32 is written in the third person. Someone else is singing this song about Israel. It does not sound as if the Jews sing this song about themselves. Therefore other people could easily sing this song. Also the description of those in the above verses would fit the Gentiles, since it is stated that they did not take the mark of the beast. We know that the mark will be forced upon people out of all nations. Again note that in Deuteronomy 32:1, Moses starts his song by addressing it to the heavens and the earth. It is a song for all to consider. Also note that at the end of the above verse, the Lord God is said to be the King of all nations, not just of Israel. Therefore the reference here to the song of Moses does not in any way prove that those who sing that song have to be Jews. There will be Gentiles out of all nations who will also be saved after refusing the mark of the beast, who will die and go to heaven. They are the same group which is mentioned in Revelation 20:4.

So now we return to Revelation chapter 14.

Revelation 14:17-20; *"And another angel came out of the temple which is in heaven, he also having a sharp sickle. And another angel came out from the altar which had **power over fire**; and cried with a loud cry to him that had the sharp sickle, saying, Thrust in thy sharp sickle, and gather the clusters of the vine of the earth; for her grapes are fully ripe. And the angel thrust in his sickle into the earth, and gathered the vine of the earth and cast [it] into the great winepress of the wrath of God. And the winepress was trodden without the city, and blood came out of the winepress, even unto the horse bridles, by the space of a thousand [and] six hundred furlongs."*

A different angel which had power over fire comes forth. He proclaims the judgment against the wicked. This angel who has the power over fire, probably ushers in the great and terrible day of the Lord. Note that this angel uses the same form of punishment as is mentioned in Isaiah 24:6; the people of the earth are burned with fire. This angel gathers only the wicked, the saved have already been taken by the Lord before that. This is the same judgment which is mentioned in Joel 3:13-14, and therefore we know that the place where the winepress mentioned here will stand is in the valley of Jehosaphat.

Isaiah 24:17-20; *"Fear, and the pit, and the snare, [are] upon thee, O inhabitant of the earth. And it shall come to pass, [that] he who fleeth from the noise of the fear shall fall into the pit; and he that cometh up out of the midst of the pit shall be taken in the snare: for the windows from on high are open, and the foundations of the earth do shake. The earth is utterly broken down, the earth is clean dissolved, the earth is moved exceedingly. The earth shall reel to and fro like a drunkard, and shall be removed like a cottage; and the transgression thereof shall be heavy upon it; and it shall fall, and not rise again."*

Isaiah likewise reports the beginning of intensified judgment, after he has reported the treachery by the wicked. Because of their wickedness, fear and the pit and a snare come upon the wicked of the earth. The judgments will be so terrible that even the very earth will break.

Isaiah 24:21-22; *"And it shall come to pass in that day, [that] the LORD shall punish the host of the high ones [that are] on high, and the kings of the earth upon the earth. And they shall be gathered together [as] prisoners are gathered in the pit, and shall be shut up in the prison, and after many days shall they be visited."*

The expression 'in that day' is a reference to the end time, which includes all of Israel's Tribulation, and the day of the Lord. Now the punishment of the wicked leaders on earth and in heaven is announced. First Satan and his fallen angels are punished by being cast out of the heavenlies into the earth (refer to Revelation 12:7-9), and a short time later the punishment is completed when they are gathered together and shut in the pit (compare with Revelation 20:1-3). Likewise the wicked leaders of this world will be punished while on earth, and then sent to the pit.

Isaiah 24:23; *"Then the moon shall be confounded, and the sun ashamed, when the LORD of hosts shall reign in mount Zion, and in Jerusalem, and before his ancients gloriously."*

At last the glorious reign of the Lord from mount Zion during the millennium is recorded. And so Isaiah completed his account of the end time, which fits in with what John reports in Revelation. Both accounts supplement each other, which **proves the inspiration** of the word of God.

This terminates **Part One** of this study. **Part Two** deals in detail with the woman of Revelation Chapter 12, along with some related issues.

Part Two

Who is the woman of Revelation Chapter 12?

One of the important chapters in the word of God in regard to prophecy is the 12th chapter of the book of Revelation. Who is the woman who stands on the moon, is clothed with the sun and wears a crown of 12 stars? The correct understanding of this prophecy is important, since it will give a clearer picture of the roles of Israel and the Church in the future. Scripture seems to bear out the fact that Israel and the Church are closely related and yet they are different. Perhaps to refer to them as sisters-in-law would not be far off the mark. For this reason it is not always easy to distinguish between the two when studying prophecy.

Many able, well educated and godly Christians have already commented on this chapter and given their interpretation. It is not surprising that before now the vision could not be fully understood because the time was not ripe. We are clearly told in Daniel 12:4 that his prophetic writings are to be shut up until the end times. It is at the time of the end that knowledge will be increased. The books of Daniel and Revelation compliment each other. Therefore since the last days of this present age have clearly arrived, we must expect that those Scriptures which until now were difficult to understand will be understood. Today, when the godless establishment media bombards Christians with falsehood, lies and deception a clear understanding of prophecy is needed for the edification of Christians. The main-line churches have to a great degree lost the clear message presented in the word of God, and no longer edify the body of Christ. To counteract all this the Holy Spirit opens up the word of prophecy to those who are earnestly seeking. Part Two is presented as a Bible study. Read it with your King James Bible open before you and check every Scripture reference given. Form your own opinion while comparing this study with the word of God. Be unbiased and first pray that the Holy Spirit will show you if these things are indeed true. If you do, then you will be blessed as is promised in Revelation 1:3.

In this study the terms 'Israel' or 'saved Jews' excludes those Jews who during the Church age have come in true repentance to Jesus Christ. Since they of course are part of the Church, they are also

Christians. The term 'Israel' refers to God's people before or after the Church age.

The Two Wives in the Bible

Before we investigate the woman of Revelation chapter 12, it will be necessary to determine into which context the two wives who are mentioned in the Bible are to be taken. We know that Israel in the Old Testament is said to be the wife of Jehovah who is married to him (Isaiah 54:5-6; Jeremiah 3:14).

It is also stated in Jeremiah 31:7 & 9 that Jehovah is the father of Jacob (Israel) and that the Jewish tribes are Jehovah's children (compare with Isaiah 64:8; 63:16; Malachi 2:10). In other words, Jehovah is the Father of the Jews and the nation of Israel is his wife. Furthermore, in Isaiah 50:1 Jehovah declares that he has not written out a bill of divorcement to the mother of the Jews, he is still married to Israel. In Hosea 2:2 (compare with Ezekiel 23:2-3) Israel, the mother of the Jews, is set aside by Jehovah. Because of her sin he rejects her as wife and refuses to be her husband. A separation has taken place. But since no bill of divorce has been written, it is not a permanent separation. Israel will be forgiven, a new covenant will be made with her, and she will be betrothed for ever to Jehovah (Hosea 2:18-19). To put it all together: Jehovah is the husband to the nation Israel and the Father of the Jews. Today they are separated, but after Israel has repented of her sin, Jehovah will make a new covenant with them and they will be married forever. Therefore Israel is the wife of Jehovah.

In the New Testament we find a different situation. Here it is revealed that the Church will be married to Jesus Christ who is the Son of God. The Church is already espoused to one husband who is Jesus Christ (Romans 7:4; 2 Corinthians 11:2; Ephesians 5:25-28). The marriage has not yet taken place. The Church today is only the bride of Christ. She is espoused (betrothed) to Him (2 Corinthians 11:2). In W.E. Vine's Expository Dictionary of New Testament Words (p.41), it is stated: "*espoused* the thought may be that of fitting or joining to one Husband, the middle voice expressing the Apostle's interest or desire in doing so." Today's expression; 'to be engaged' would come close to the intended meaning of 2 Corinthians 11:2. The marriage according to Revelation 19:7-16 will take place some time after the rapture but before the return of Christ as King to earth. The future role of the Church as the wife of Christ is partly explained in Ephesians 5:22-33).

1. The wife has to submit to her husband.

2. The Church (wife) will be glorious not having spot or wrinkle.

3. Husband and wife shall be one flesh (or one body).

4. The wife must reverence her husband.

5. And according to Genesis 2:18 the wife is meant to be the helpmeet (helper) for her husband.

Therefore the Church as the wife of Christ will be one flesh with him, she will be glorious and therefore brings honour and glory to her husband. The Church will be submissive to Christ who loves her like his own body. The Church will be Christ's helper in all his offices. e.g. as King and Priest. If we keep these points in mind, the future role of the Church as the wife of Christ the King will be easier understood. Now let us have a look at the marriage of the Lamb.

The Marriage of the Lamb

Revelation 19:7-9; *"Let us be glad and rejoice, and give honour to him: for the marriage of the Lamb is come, and his wife hath made herself ready. And to her was granted that she should be arrayed in fine linen, clean and white: for the fine linen is the righteousness of saints."*

It is stated that the Lamb was married to his wife. The Lamb is, of course, Jesus Christ, the Son of God. As already shown above, we know that it is the Church who will be married to the Lord Jesus. Let's see how this is confirmed here and in later chapters. The first clue is given by stating that his wife has made herself ready. She is worthy to become the wife of the holy Son of God. This fits the description of the Church. The Church has been washed with the blood of the Lamb, and she will be presented as a chaste virgin (2 Corinthians 11:2). Also since the saints by this time would have appeared before the Judgement seat of Christ (2 Corinthians 5:10; Romans 14:10), we can see that indeed the Church has made herself ready. The next clue is that the wife is arrayed in white linen which is the righteousness of the saints. Christians are saints who will be clothed in white raiment (Revelation 3:4-5; 3:18; 4:4). Therefore these two clues indicate that the Church is the wife of the Lamb. The next mention of the bride the Lamb's wife is in chapter 21.

Revelation chapter 21 and onwards deals with the eternal state of God's kingdom. John wrote: *"And I saw a new heaven and a new earth:"* pointing us to the time after the 1,000 year millennium. He continues in verse two: "A*nd I John saw the holy city, new Jerusalem, coming down from God out of Heaven, prepared as a bride adorned for her husband.*" Note, he does not say that the city is the bride, but rather the city was prepared in the same way as a bride prepares herself for her husband. The emphasis here is on the fact that the city has been prepared. The Lord Jesus said to his disciples before he left them, that he would go to prepare a place for them (John 14:2). Now this city is the place which he had prepared. The Lord prepared the city in the same way as a bride would prepare herself for her husband. In the best possible way.

Next in Revelation 21:9, the angel says that he is going to show the Lamb's wife to John. Remember the time into which John in his spirit is projected is after the millennium. By this time the Church, the wife of the Lamb, would have been living in the new Jerusalem for about 1,000 years. John in his spirit has been projected to about 2,000 and 3,000 years into the future. He is a time traveller. But this causes some problems. How can he report events which he sees happening, yet are 3,000 years in the future beyond his own time, and then record them in such a way that generations future from his time still understand? He has to cover five different ages. His own age, the age between his and the Tribulation, the time during the Tribulation leading up to the millennium, the millennium itself, and finally the eternal state. For this reason it is sometimes difficult to know which age he is referring to in his writings.

John is transported to a great and high mountain, from where he could observe the city come down out of heaven. John reports that he saw the Great City. If the city itself was the Lamb's wife, John would have said so. But instead he said that he saw the Great City descending out of heaven. He did not say that he saw the Lamb's wife descending out of heaven. John quite naturally, reported first the externals, that which he saw first, of that breathtaking city. After describing the external appearance of the city, he turns his attention to the internals, and it is there where he sees the wife of the Lamb. The first mention John makes to what is the wife is in Revelation 21:27, those which are inside the city are those which are written in the Lamb's book of life. We know that this must refer to Christians since the names of all Christians are written in the book of life (Philippians 4:3; Revelations 3:5).

Revelation 22:3 gives the next reference as to what the wife is. Here it is stated that the Lamb's servants are inside the city. The Lamb's servants in the book of Revelation are Christians, this is made clear right at the outset in chapter one; in verses one and four it is written: "*The Revelation of Jesus Christ, which God gave unto him, to show unto his servants things which must shortly come to pass; and he sent and signified it by his angel unto his servant John. ..... John to the seven churches which are in Asia*:" The whole book of Revelation was given to the Church, to the servants of Jesus Christ to know what the future for them would bring. This is confirmed in the last chapter, where the Lord states that he had sent his angel so that John would be able to testify those things which were shown to him in the churches. These statements make it clear, that the Church was meant to be the main recipient of the book of Revelation.

That these servants inside the City must be Christians is also indicated by the statement: "*And they shall see his face*." this is the same language as in 1 Corinthians 13:12, where it is stated: "*For now we see through a glass darkly, but then face to face*."

Again, the statement (Revelation 22:4): "*and his name shall be in their foreheads*." points to the fact that here it is Christians who are under consideration. Compare this with Revelation 3:12, where Christ promises the overcoming Christian: "*I will write upon him MY new name*." It is Jesus Christ's new name that will be written upon the overcoming Christian. All this indicates that the servants of Revelation 22:3-5 are Christians who make up the wife of Christ.

There are other servants mentioned in the book of Revelation who have a name written in their foreheads. These are the 144,000 virgins of

Revelation 14:1. It is not the name of Christ but of the Father which is written in their foreheads, and so a clear distinction between the two groups is made.

The next hint that the wife of the Lamb is present in the City, is given in 22:3 & 5. The servants are assembled near the throne of God, with the Lamb sitting in it, then it is stated: *"and they shall reign forever and ever."* In Revelation 3:21, the Lord promises the Christian: *"To him that overcometh will I grant to sit with me on my throne."* (Compare also with 2 Timothy 2:12). Therefore we can see that the servants in these verses must indeed by Christians, who make up the Lamb's wife.

In contrast to the Church, which will reign forever and ever, the resurrected Tribulation saints shall only reign (on earth) for 1,000 years (Revelation 20:6).

Again in Revelation 22:14, it is confirmed that those which have a right to be in the city must be Christians, and that therefore the wife of the Lamb is indeed inside the city and John saw her there. Those inside the city have a right to the tree of life. Compare that with Revelation 2:7.

The final indication that the Church, the bride of Christ, is inside the city, is given in Revelation 22:16-17. The Lord Jesus said that all that has been shown was to be testified in the churches. If Israel is the wife of the Lamb (as some people claim), then why should this be testified to the churches? Would it not make more sense to have it testified inside the synagogues? Therefore as at the start of the book of Revelation, likewise at the end, it is stated that the book was written for the benefit, edification and education of the Church. For this reason we should expect that the reported events in Revelation primarily concern the Church. Israel's future was foretold in the Olivet discourse.

In the epilogue of Revelation 22:6-17, there is a brief summary of the most important issues. It is difficult to determine the point of time to which these verses refer. Is it a pre or post marriage setting? The Church now speaks as the bride of Christ. She invites the present day sinner to come. It is as if she said, I will be there inside the heavenly city, if you want to be part of this, then come. Come in true repentance to the foot of the cross. She gives an invitation to sinners of previous ages, to come in true repentance to Christ, to join the Church. Today sinners can still, through repentance, become part of the bride of the Lamb.

The Wife of Christ a Queen?

Scripture bears out the fact, that the citizenship of the Church is in heaven. (Philippians 3:20) *"For our conversation (citizenship) is in heaven; from whence also we look for the Saviour, the Lord Jesus Christ"*. Compare with Ephesians 2:19. Here on earth Christians are ambassadors (2 Corinthians 5:20), we belong to a different country. Also 1 Peter 2:11 mentions the same fact that we are only strangers and pilgrims here on earth. We are only sojourners, only here for a temporary stay (1 Peter 1:17). Our citizenship is not of this world but of heaven.

Christians are a heavenly people. The Lord Jesus went away to prepare a place for his Church, his future wife. This place or home is in heaven. Consequently the future destiny and role of the Church has to be sought in the heavenlies, not on earth. This is one of the reasons why a Christian should not fix his eyes and desires on the things of the world, but on heavenly things, since his home will be there. As such whenever we try to understand the future of the Church, we must always keep this heavenly role in mind. The Lord Jesus said to Pilate: *"My Kingdom is not of the world: .... but now is my Kingdom not from hence."* (John 18:36). This clearly indicates that the Kingdom of which Christ will be King involves far more than this world. His is a heavenly kingdom. As was shown before, the Church is destined to become the wife of Christ, who is the Lamb of God and King of kings. Hence one of the roles of the Church will be to be the 'helpmeet', of her husband the King. The Church as wife has to help Christ in his offices as King and Priest. The Christians are said to be a royal priesthood (1 Peter 2:9). All this may indicate that the Church has to fulfil the functions of a heavenly queen, with all her duties.

A duty of a queen is to help in ruling. This idea may be hinted at in 1 Corinthians 6:2. One of the definitions for the word 'judge' (Greek 'krino'), according to some scholars is "to govern" or "to rule". The definition for the word 'world' (Greek 'kosmos') is 'Universe'. If these definitions are then inserted into 1 Corinthians 6:2-3, it would read like this:

*"Do ye not know that the saints shall **rule** the **universe**? and if the **universe** be **ruled** by you, are ye unworthy to **rule** the smallest matters?*

*Know ye not that we shall **rule** angels? how much more things that pertain to this life?"*

If this interpretation is accepted, then it would support the idea of a heavenly role for a Church royal.

Another duty for a queen is to glorify the King. This is indirectly indicated in 1 Peter 2:9; where the Church members are exhorted: *"that ye should shew forth the praises of him who has called you out of darkness into his marvellous light:"* The same thought is expressed in Ephesians 5:27.

That the Church may be a queen under Christ the King is a fact not readily seen in Scripture, and can only be concluded when looking at several Scriptures together. It is not a doctrine which has any bearing on salvation, but could enlighten and edify those Christians who desire to find out some deeper truth in the word of God. Christians will have different understandings on the subject, but should not let it become a contentious issue.

Here are some reasons why the Church could be seen as a heavenly queen.

1. She will become wife to the King, as such she would be a queen.

2. Christians who make up the Church are said to be a royal priesthood. 1 Peter 2: 9.

3. One of the wife's roles in Scripture is to be the helpmeet of her husband. As such one of her duties should be to help in ruling and governing. This is one service predicted in Scripture for the Christians, who collectively make up the Church. This is a duty which a queen, of course, would also have to perform.

4. The wife is to submit to her husband, just as the Church is subject unto Christ (Ephesians 5:21-24). The scriptural example of the wife was performed by Sarah, who called her husband Lord (1 Peter 3:6). This seems to convey the reverence which a queen has towards the King.

5. An important role for a queen is to bring glory and honour to the King, just as the Church is exhorted to do. I Peter 2:9; Eph. 5:27.

6. In Revelation chapter 12 the woman representing the visible Church (as will be shown later) is said to wear a crown. Does this give us a clue about the Church being a queen?

7. Psalm 45 speaks about Christ the King. Then in verse 9 it states that the queen stands at his right hand. Could the queen here refer to the Church, Christ's wife? (Refer to the chapter **'The Church in Psalm 45'**).

8. Jeremiah (7:18) mentions a false queen of heaven. Could this queen of heaven be Satan's counterfeit? We know that Satan is the great imitator of God:

   a. Satan imitated the cross. The symbol of the cross was used as a pagan religious symbol long before the Lord died on one. (Ref. **'The two Babylons'** pages 198-200, by Hislop)

   b. Satan imitates God's light and the seven candlesticks of Revelation 1:20, by using candles in religious services.

   c. Satan imitated Christ in his role as **'The Sun of Righteousness'**: (Malachi 4:2), and also the Saints who shall **'shine forth as the sun'** (Matthew 13:43). This he does by having initiated sun worship.

   d. Satan imitates the gifts of the Holy Spirit by introducing false tongues.

   e. Satan imitates God's kingdom by ruling as king over his own earthly kingdom (Matthew 12:26).

   f. Satan imitates the **'Gospel of Grace'** by introducing his gospel of 'Salvation by works'.

   g. Satan imitates the Biblical doctrine of life eternal by preaching reincarnation.

   h. And Satan imitates the woman and the 'man-child' of Revelation chapter 12 by setting up, all over the world, his own mother and child images (Ref. **'Babylon, Mystery Religion'** p.8 by R.E. Woodrow). The mother with child is said to be the 'wife of Baal (sun), the virgin queen of heaven'.

The question is, why would Satan bother to set up a false queen of Heaven? Could the reason be that there will be a true heavenly queen, whom he wants to imitate in order to confuse people? All the above points are only indirect evidence. But they do add weight to the interpretation of Revelation chapter 12, as given in this study.

It should be remembered that the Lord Jesus fulfils several offices. For example, he is called the Lion of Judah but also a Lamb. His role as a Lion is obviously different from that of a Lamb. Likewise the Church, she in her role as a bride or wife would have to differ from her possible role as a queen. The husband-wife relationship is that of an intimate loving, trusting personal one, just as the relationship which is shown in Scripture to exist between Christ and the Church. However when the King with his Queen comes forth in royal apparel, their relationship would be seen to be different. The Queen would be seen to be in respectful submissiveness to the King. Such a respectful relationship for the Christian towards God is indicated in the following Scriptures. 2 Corinthians 7:1; Ephesians 5:21; Philippians 2:12-13. Another Scripture which indicates the same is Hebrews 12:28-29, "*Wherefore we receiving a kingdom which cannot be moved, let us have grace, whereby we may serve God acceptably with reverence and godly fear: For our God is a consuming fire*". Here the Greek word for fear is '*eulabeia*' meaning reverence, dread fear. This relationship of a servant who reveres his master would be similar to that of a queen to her king. Do these different relationships between the Church and Christ indicate the different offices which are purposed for the Church?

Is the future role of the Church as queen thus foreshadowed? The Lord Jesus said to his disciples; "*I have yet many things to say unto you, but ye cannot bear them now*." (John 16:12). Also the Lord said to Nicodemus in John 3:12, "*If I have told you earthly things, and ye believe not, how shall ye believe, if I tell you of heavenly things*?" Likewise today's Christians may not be able to fully comprehend heavenly realities. Perhaps for this reason the Bible speaks little about heavenly facts, or about the future role of the Church. Christians today may not be able to fully comprehend how we are going to serve our Lord and God in days to come. Maybe for this reason the office of the Church as queen is only indicated in an indirect way. God may not want us to focus too much on a subject which we at this stage cannot fully comprehend.

To summarise: Israel is the wife of Jehovah the Father. They are at this point of time separated, but will be reunited forever and ever. The true Church consisting of all those who are born again, is today the bride, but will become the wife of Christ the Son of God. Christ is King of kings who will rule with his 'helpmeet' forever and ever, (Revelation 22:5). Since Christ the husband is King, the Church his wife could be queen. It follows then, since Christ's Kingdom is not of this world, but of a heavenly kingdom, the Church if she indeed will be queen, would therefore have to be a heavenly queen. This will become clearer, when Revelation chapter 12 is considered. In contrast to a true queen, Satan has set up his false queen of Heaven.

The Church in Psalm 45

This Psalm outlines briefly the situation after the Tribulation, that is during the interval between the Tribulation and the second coming. Its main purpose is to show the glory and majesty of Christ the King. But also the Church and saved Israel are shown in their future glory.

v. 1-2; *"My heart is inditing a good matter: I speak of the things which I have made touching the king: my tongue is the pen of a ready writer. Thou art fairer than the children of men: grace is poured into thy lips: therefore God hath blessed thee forever."*

The beauty of Christ is described; he is fairer than any other human being.

v. 3; *"Gird thy sword upon thy thigh, O most mighty, with thy glory and thy majesty."*

Now Christ the King is exhorted to prepare himself for battle with his enemies.

v. 4; *"And in thy majesty ride prosperously because of truth and meekness and righteousness; and thy right hand shall teach thee terrible things."*

The Lord is asked to ride victoriously. This ties in with Revelation 19:11-16. There the Lord is said to sit upon a white horse, and is called *"Faithful and true, and in righteousness he does judge and make war.*" Clearly the same event is in view in both passages. The Revelation passages leave no doubt that the time of this event is shortly before the second coming of Christ as King. This tells us into which time slot to place Psalm 45.

v. 5; *"Thine arrows are sharp in the heart of the king's enemies; whereby the people fall under thee."*

Here the result of the war is indicated, the enemies of Christ the King fall.

v. 6; *"Thy throne, O God, is forever and ever: the sceptre of thy kingdom is a right sceptre."*

The kingdom of which Christ is King is an everlasting kingdom (compare with Psalm 93).

v. 7; *"Thou lovest righteousness, and hatest wickedness: therefore God, thy God, hath anointed thee with the oil of gladness above thy fellows."*

Because of our Lord's righteousness, he is exalted above all.

v. 8; *"All thy garments smell of myrrh, and aloes, and cassis, out of the ivory palaces, whereby they have made thee glad."*

The spices mentioned here are the same as those which were used while our Lord was prepared for burial (John 19:39-40). Therefore the symbolism in this Psalm points to his double ministry, to that as a lion and also to that as a lamb.

v. 9; *"Kings' daughters were among thy honourable women: upon thy right hand did stand the queen in gold of Ophir."*

The 'King James Bible' doesn't translate the first half of the verse as well as Luther has done in his German translation. Luther's German translation reads:

"In deinem Schmuck gehen der Konige Tochter;" which translated into English reads:

"Kings' daughters walk with your adornment." This translation, as

shall be shown, fits the context better. But who are those Kings' daughters?

Psalm 9:14; *"That I may shew forth all thy praise in the gates of the daughter of Zion: I will rejoice in thy salvation."*

Isaiah 1:8; *"And the daughter of Zion is left as a cottage in a vineyard, as a lodge in a garden of cucumbers, as a besieged city."*

Isaiah 23:10 & 12; *"Pass through thy land as a river, O daughter of Tar-shish there is no more strength. And he said, Thou shalt no more rejoice, O thou oppressed virgin, daughter of Zidon: arise, pass over to Chittim; there also shalt thou have no rest."*

These verses show that a daughter in a prophetic context represents a company of people. This is confirmed in Isaiah 47:1; Jeremiah 6:2 etc. (A virgin daughter would be a people which so far have not been disturbed).

Kings' daughters are those born to a king. According to Revelation 1:6; and 1 Peter 2:9 Christians are already kings (that is in the spiritual realm).

"And hath made us kings and priests unto God and his Father; to him be glory and dominion forever and ever, Amen."

Also those who come to Christ through the witness of a Christian are his children in the Lord. The Christian in a way is their spiritual father. That, together with the fact that Christians have God as Father in heaven who is King of all, makes them truly the children of a king. Therefore an assembly of true believers are children of kings. They have been born again, and have a new father who is King.

1 Corinthians 4:15; *"For though ye have ten thousand instructors in Christ, yet have ye not many fathers: for in Christ Jesus I have begotten you through the gospel."*

2 Corinthians 6:13; *"Now for a recompence in the same, (I speak as unto my children,) be ye also enlarged."*

1 Thessalonians 2:11-12; *"As ye know how we exhorted and comforted and charged every one of you, as a father doth his children. That ye*

would walk worthy of God, who hath called you unto his kingdom and glory."

1 John 2:1; *"My little children, these things write I unto you, that ye sin not. And if any man sin, we have an advocate with the Father, Jesus Christ the righteous."*

The various assemblies are therefore daughters of kings. That a Christian assembly is seen to be a daughter (or lady, or sister) is confirmed in 2 John verses 1 and 13.

2 John 1 & 13; *"The elder unto the elect lady and her children, whom I love in the truth; and not I only, but also all they that have known the truth; .... The children of thy elect sister greet thee. Amen."*

The elect lady to which John addresses his letter is obviously a local church. This **'elect lady'** has an **'elect sister'**, which must be some other local church.

An *'elect lady'* which is John's terminology seems to be the same as a 'kings' daughter', the term used in Psalm 45.

Now the King's daughters of verse 9, according to Luther, wear the king's adornment (his righteousness). The queen which did stand at the right hand of Christ the King is said to be adorned in gold of O'phir. The queen here must be the King's wife, that is, the Church. Out of her would have come all the King's daughters (the various assemblies) from the entire Church age. Therefore this Psalm seems to confirm that the Church will become the queen of Christ the King.

It should be noted that since the daughters wear the Lord's adornment, it is only fitting for the queen to stand in gold of Ophir. What does gold symbolise?

Malachi 3:3; *"And he shall sit as a refiner and purifier of silver: and he shall purify the sons of Levi, and purge them as gold and silver, that they may offer unto the Lord an offering in righteousness."*

Revelation 3:18; *"I counsel thee to buy of me gold tried in the fire, that thou mayest be rich; and white raiment, that thou mayest be clothed, and that the shame of thy nakedness do not appear; and anoint thine eyes with eyesalve, that thou mayest see."*

It is generally accepted that in Scripture gold is symbolic for purity. Therefore the queen here is said to be adorned with the purity (or righteousness) of Christ the King, certainly a description which fits the Church.

The statement that the queen *'did stand'* at the right hand of the King can be significant, since the time of which this Psalm speaks seems to be between the end of Israel's Tribulation and the second coming of Christ with all his saints.

At that time Christ is said to ride on his horse to wage war against his enemies and before that event, the marriage of the Lamb would have taken place. At the marriage, his wife (the Church) would of course have to stand on his right hand, therefore Revelation chapter 3 and Psalm 45 seem to convey the same message. But how does the rest of the Psalm fit into the picture?

v. 10; *"Hearken, O daughter, and consider, and incline thine ear; forget also thine own people, and thy father's house;"*

In this verse the spotlight is turned to a *specific* daughter, she is not yet a king's daughter. She does not have to be part of those daughters mentioned in verse 9. She can be a different daughter altogether, a different company of people. Before this daughter is accepted by the King, she must first fulfil certain conditions.

1. **She must consider**. Consider what? Well if this daughter represents the surviving Jews after the Tribulation (compare Lamentations 1:6), then they must consider the claim by Christ to be their Messiah.

2. **She must listen** to those who have already believed in Christ, and consider their testimony and the word of God.

3. **She must forget** her own generation of the people of Israel. Her loyalty has to shift from her people to Christ. This exhortation is the same as given by our Lord in Luke 17:31. There the Jews are admonished not to go down into their house, when they see that the Son of man is coming. If they do, then they prove that worldly goods or concerns are more important to them than the opportunity to meet the Lord.

v. 11; *"So shall the king greatly desire thy beauty: for he is thy Lord;*

and worship thou him."

The Jews are promised that if they meet the conditions of verse 10, then Christ will gladly have them. The daughter is reminded that Christ is indeed their Lord and they must worship him.

v. 12; "*And the daughter of Tyre shall be there with a gift; even the rich among the people shall entreat thy favour.*"

During the millennium the Gentile nations will give favours to the Jews. The people of Tyre may again (as during the construction of Solomon's temple) assist Israel in the construction or beautification of a new temple. Also the rich (kings and nobles) of the nations shall bring gifts to receive Israel's favour (compare with Psalm 68:28-31).

v. 13; "*The king's daughter is all glorious within: her clothing is of wrought gold.*"

The setting of the time of Psalm 45 changes to the millennium. By now Israel has been accepted as a king's daughter. She also, just as the Church, is adorned with gold. She has repented and is glorious within, which means that the Holy Spirit is inside the Jewish believers.

v. 14; "*She shall be brought unto the king in raiment of needlework: the virgins her companions that follow her shall be brought unto thee.*"

Israel will be presented to the King; the virgins (could they be the 14,000 virgins of Revelation 14:4?) will also be brought unto Christ.

v. 15; "*With gladness and rejoicing shall they be brought: they shall enter into the King's palace.*"

They will all enter with gladness and rejoicing into the King's palaces; this could be a reference to the new Jerusalem.

v. 16; "*Instead of thy fathers shall be thy children, whom thou mayest make princes in all the earth.*"

Israel should not focus on the past, they should not look to their fathers, that is Jacob and his 12 sons. It is their children who will become great on earth, thus indicating again that Israel's promises are to be fulfilled on earth.

v. 17; *"I will make thy name to be remembered in all generations; therefore shall the people praise thee forever and ever."*

All glory will go to Christ.

Now we will consider Revelation chapter 12.

Who is the Woman with the Man-Child of Revelation 12 ?

Revelation 12:1; *"And there appeared a great wonder in heaven; a woman clothed with the sun, and the moon under her feet, and upon her head a crown of twelve stars:"*

The expression **'a great wonder'** could just as well be translated **'a great sign'**, as some translations have done. As the woman is standing on the moon she would have to be in the sky or cosmos, but not in heaven, the abode of God. The Greek word used here is 'ouranos' which equally correctly can mean 'sky'. Therefore another translation could read **'a great sign in the sky'**. A sign in the sky cannot be hidden from the world, but can be seen by all, even if not understood by all. As such, whatever the woman of Revelation 12:1 stands for can be seen by the world. The woman and her meaning are symbolical, but what she represents is not, and this can be seen by all.

The scene in Revelation chapter 12 is symbolical, since no literal woman can be clothed with the sun, and stand on the moon. Hence the term 'man-child' with the rest of the vision, has also to be understood in a symbolical manner. However to ensure a correct interpretation, every aspect of the 'sign' has to fit the picture, and has to find support from other Scripture passages. Three interpretations are to be considered.

1. The woman as seen by the world represents the visible Church of the whole Church age, while the 'man-child' represents the body of Christ (all true believers) at the time of the rapture.

2. The woman represents Israel, and the 'man-child' the baby Jesus.

3. The woman represents Mary queen of heaven as is taught by Roman Catholicism.

We shall now consider every aspect of the vision verse by verse to determine which interpretation best fits the picture. The correct interpretation must harmonise in every detail with the given facts.

To be correct, the following points and others have to be explained, and must fit the overall picture.

1. The woman is clothed with the sun.

2. She has the moon under her feet.

3. She wears a crown of 12 stars.

4. She is with child.

5. She travails and is in pain to give birth.

6. The dragon wants to devour the child as soon as it is born.

7. She brings forth a 'man-child', who will rule with a rod of iron.

8. The child is caught up to God and his throne.

9. The woman flees into the wilderness, to a place prepared for her.

10. The woman has other children.

11. Satan will persecute the woman and her other children.

First, an explanation of the identity of the woman in this prophecy. The sign of the woman in the sky is meant to convey the picture of the visible Church as it is seen by the world. The woman herself is not the Church; she represents that which God has purposed for the whole Church. Only the child in her is the true Church as seen by God, and only the child will inherit that which was meant for all. In the same way all of Israel could have inherited the promised land, but only the new generation did finally inherit it. It may not be obvious, but the Church according to Revelation includes Roman Catholicism (Thyatira) and apostate Protestantism (Laodecia). As already mentioned in Part One of this study, the letters to the seven Churches, from Revelation 2:1 to the end of chapter 3, are also, after an initial address to those actual churches, an outline of the history of the Church age.

A church holds her position as a light bearer only so long as true believers are still in her. In Revelation 1:12 to 2:5 it is indicated that a faithful Church is represented by a candlestick (i.e., lampstand), but if the Church loses her witness or testimony, her lampstand is removed and she is no longer a giver of light. Consequently a Church which loses all her true believers has lost her witness, her light, and her glory. Roman Catholicism (Thyatira) and apostate Protestantism (Laodecia) are included amongst the churches because there are still, and always have been, some true believers in them. But as soon as the true believers are removed by the rapture from the visible Church, the light and the glorious position of the Church is also removed, and what is left is an assembly of religious people. As such the woman represents all churches of all ages, as outlined in the book of Revelation, regardless of whether they have been good or bad churches.

The term '**visible Church**' as used in this study, means the Church as a whole as perceived and seen by the world. The visible Church includes all those which are in any way connected to a Christian organisation. They include the saved and unsaved alike. It is not the true Church, since the true Church consists only of born again believers. At the time of the rapture when all true Christians have been removed from the visible Church, she will remain only an assembly of religious people. At that point of time she is no longer recognised by God as a church at all. That may be the reason why the word of God describes the visible Church as a woman, rather than a church. She is not the Church, but the Church is in her, just as a daughter in prophecy sometimes symbolises a company of people, which includes the saved and unsaved. However, even after the departure of the true Church the world will still see the woman as being the Church. Out of this woman will come other true believers, but they will no longer be part of the Church, they will serve God in a different way. They are those which are commonly referred to as the tribulation Saints.

The Woman is Clothed with the Sun

Revelation 12:1; *"And there appeared a great wonder in heaven; a woman clothed with the sun, and the moon under her feet, and upon her head a crown of twelve stars:"*

A principle of the New Testament is that the individual Christian forms part of the body of Christ. Romans 12:5; *"We, being many, are one body in Christ, and every one members one of another."* (Compare with 1 Corinthians 10:17). As such instructions, exhortations or doctrines which are directed to one Christian are normally applicable to the whole Church, (for example, if some are exhorted to be the light of the world, then the whole Church is exhorted to be the light of the world). If the Church is said to be a lampstand, then each single member of the body should be a light bearer.

The primary function of the sun is to provide light. As such, whenever the sun is mentioned in a symbolical context, the explanation of the symbol must have reference to the light of the sun. The visible Church has always been seen to be the holder of light and to be the overcomer of darkness. The members of the Church were told to be the light of the world (Matthew 5:14; Colossians 1:12) and the seven candlesticks of Revelation 1:20, which represent the complete Church, are a picture of the Church bringing light into the world. Also Philippians 2:15 states that Christians shine as lights in the world. Now to a greater or lesser degree the visible Church (if only because of the true believers in her) has been able to bring light into the world. The light was the gospel light, and the truth of the word of God, delivered by the Church to the world. Even Christians helped in this effort. The light of the gospel brings light and liberty and overcomes darkness. The fact that the woman is 'clothed' with the sun is also significant. Clothes are worn externally; they are not a permanent part of the person wearing them. They will be put off again. The light which the woman wears is not a permanent feature of her, it is only put on and temporal. The temporal light of the woman is in contrast to the permanent light of the righteous, who will be shining forth as the sun (Matthew 13:43). The light of the righteous will come out from within. The woman however is only clothed with the light. This light she will lose as soon as the true believers are taken out of her. Therefore the picture of the woman being clothed with the sun is a fitting description of the visible Church being the light bearer of the world.

The Woman has the Moon under her Feet

As much as the sun rules the day, the moon rules the night (Psalm 136:9). The light of the moon is weak and without life. It is not able to overcome the darkness. During the rule of the moon the deeds of the forces of darkness are performed. The moon has some light, but it is not overcoming light, not life giving light, like that of the sun. Moonlight is dim, cold and lifeless, exactly as the light of false pagan religions. Pagan religions do have some understanding and knowledge which can sometimes help a person. But the light that false religions have does not bring life. Its adherents are still in darkness and lost. Therefore the moon is a good symbol of man's false pagan religions. Also we must not forget that in witchcraft and in many pagan religions the moon holds a special place, and is often adored and even worshipped. (Ref. 2 Kings 23:5; Jeremiah 8:2.)

The visible Church was able, on the whole throughout its existence, to overcome pagan religions and witchcraft wherever it went. Again it should be emphasised that the visible Church includes Catholicism. As such, especially in former days, the woman was often ruthless when dealing with paganism. It should be noted, however, that the Bible does not endorse the actions of the woman, in fact it does not even mention them. The morality of the woman is not under consideration. She holds her celestial position only because of the child in her. The true believers inside the visible Church never used brutal methods to force their religion upon others. As soon as the child is gone, the woman's glory and privileged positions are also gone. Thus, the woman having the moon under her feet is a fitting description of the visible church standing over pagan religions suppressing them. But it would also indicate that the role which the woman has to play is a heavenly one, since her location is in space.

The Kingdom of Heaven

We now consider what the Scriptures have to say about the coming **kingdom of heaven**. The word of God has much to say about the **kingdom of heaven**. There are at least two aspects concerning it. One sheds light on the spiritual side of it. The Lord referred to that in Luke 17:21; *"The kingdom of God is within you."* The other side shows the literal aspect of it. There is indeed a kingdom to come which has its roots in heaven.

In Matthew 4:17 it is stated that Jesus began to preach *"Repent: for the kingdom of heaven is at hand."* God's kingdom was to be introduced at that time. However the nation of Israel first had to be made fit to be part of it. They first had to repent, and the land and nation had to be cleansed. John the Baptist who came first, and the Apostles who were sent out later, preached repentance. Also there was the spiritual side which had to be taken care of. The unclean spirits had to be cast out.

The Lord began to cleanse the kingdom from all demons. Matthew 12:26; *"But if I cast out devils by the Spirit of God, **then the kingdom of God is come unto you.** Or else how can one enter into a strong man's house, and spoil his goods, except he first bind the strong man? and then he will spoil his house."*

The Lord Jesus entered into Satan's kingdom (Matthew 12:26), and began to bind Satan, the strong man, along with his demonic forces, in order to defeat his satanic kingdom and cleanse the land for the kingdom of God. When the Lord began this process, the Jews should have known the sign of the times, and should have realised that the kingdom of God had come. They had no excuse. But they rejected Christ the King and with him the kingdom. Therefore this cleansing of the land from unclean spirits will not be accomplished until the time of the second coming (Zechariah 13:2).

Matthew 11:12; *"And from the days of John the Baptist until now the kingdom of heaven suffereth violence, and the violent take it by force."*

Luke 16:14-16; *"And the Pharisees also, who were covetous, heard all these things: and they derided him. And he said unto them, Ye are they which justify yourselves before men; but God knoweth your hearts: for that which is highly esteemed among men is abomination in the sight of God. The law and the prophets [were] until John:*

since that time the kingdom of God is preached, and every man presseth into it."

The kingdom had come, but those with the wrong motives tried to force themselves into it, by joining those who followed Christ. They wanted to be part of the kingdom for human reasons. However, those reasons were an abomination to God, and because of these motives the kingdom suffered.

"Therefore say I unto you, The kingdom of God shall be taken from you, and given to a nation bringing forth the fruits thereof." (Matthew 21:43). The kingdom which was theirs was to be taken from the Jews and given to another nation. The Greek word for nation here is 'ethnos' meaning Gentile people. In other words, the kingdom would be given to a nation (the Church) which consisted primarily of people from the Gentile nations. Peter referred to this when he called the church: *"A peculiar people, a holy nation."* (1 Peter 2:9). And so the kingdom was taken from the Jews and given to the Church. God's kingdom in its heavenly aspect has been given to the Church. The Jews however, when they repent, will also become part of this kingdom. Their future will be on earth. It appears that Israel will have a different function in that kingdom from that which was originally intended. The kingdom of God will basically be a heavenly kingdom as is stated in John 18:36. As such it fits the Church, a heavenly people who are translated into the kingdom of Christ Jesus, the Son of God (Colossians 1:13).

The woman of Revelation 12 stands in heaven, as a sign that the true Church in her will, as wife, be part of this kingdom. The woman stands for that which the whole Church was meant to inherit. Just as Israel in the wilderness received promises which were intended for all, but only enjoyed by their children (refer to the chapter **'Israel in the wilderness a type of the woman'**.)

It should be mentioned that just as the nation of Israel had to be cleansed from satanic forces before God's Kingdom could be fully introduced, likewise the heavenlies will have to be cleansed from Satan and his fallen angels before the Kingdom of Christ and his Church can come in its full strength. We will refer to that when Revelations 12:10 is considered.

She Wears a Crown of 12 Stars

In common understanding a woman who wears a crown must be a queen. The Lord is King of kings, and the Church will be his wife. And the wife of a King is a queen. Hence a queen who stands in Heaven must be a heavenly queen. A crown is always a sign of royalty and authority. The Bible referring to the Church states:

"*But ye are a chosen generation, a royal priesthood, an holy nation, a peculiar people; that ye should shew forth the praises of him who hath called you out of darkness into his marvellous light.*" (I Peter 2:9).

A queen is meant to show forth the praises and glory of the king, her husband. Christians will receive crowns and will sit with Christ on his throne (1 Corinthians 9:25, 1 Peter 5:4; Revelation 3:21). Therefore the woman's crown indicates the role which the whole Church was meant to enjoy, but which only her child, the true Church will in fact receive. And it fits the destiny of the Church. As such the crown of 12 stars is symbolic of the coming role of the true Church. Also the true Christians inside the visible Church are already said to be kings and priests (Revelation 1:6). Consequently it is fitting for the woman to wear the crown. Let's explain the symbols.

According to the law of first mention a symbolic star represents a minister from heaven (someone who serves or is a messenger). "*a star shall come out of Jacob, and a sceptre shall rise out of Israel,*" (Numbers 24:17). This is a prophecy about the Lord Jesus foreshadowing his ministry at his first and second coming. When he first came he was a messenger proclaiming the kingdom to come (Matthew 4:17), and a minister from God (Matthew 20:28). When he returns he will fulfil his office as King, and will have a sceptre. This gives us the clue that a star in a symbolic context represents a minister from heaven. Angels or stars are God's ministering spirits (Hebrew 1:14). A further Scripture which sheds light on this subject is Revelation 1:20, there it is stated that stars are angels who serve God by ministering to the Churches. The number 12 symbolises Government, that is why there had to be 12 apostles. They will be part of God's government in the coming kingdom (Matthew 19:28). This means that the crown of 12 stars symbolises the role of the Church in God's future kingdom, the Kingdom of heaven.

There will be 12 ministers out of the Church, ruling (under Christ) as Kings. Perhaps these 12 ministers are half of the 24 elders in Revelation 4:4, representing the Church, wearing crowns and sitting on governmental seats round about the throne of God in heaven.

The Woman was with Child

Rev. 12:2; *"And she being with child cried, travailing in birth, and pained to be delivered."*

If the woman is a symbol of a large body of people (the visible Church), then her child must likewise be a symbol of a smaller body of people (the true Church). A birth always reproduces something of the same kind. In this case out of a large body of people comes forth a smaller body of people. They are different, but still of the same kind. The birth represents a sudden separation, which is a good picture of the rapture, when all true believers will be caught up to meet the Lord in the air. It is not possible that a symbolical woman can give birth to a literal child, which would be the case if Israel and the child Jesus were here in view. Because of this fact, it is the Church rather than Israel, which fits better with the symbol of the woman in the sky.

The woman is in pain to be delivered. The visible Church today is in pain, since many of the true believers in her want to get out because of her apostasy. This causes pain and stress. This symbolism also fits the visible Church.

A Great Red Dragon

Revelation 12:3; *"And there appeared another wonder in heaven; and behold a great red dragon, having seven heads and ten horns, and seven crowns upon his heads"*

The red dragon is of course the Devil or Satan of verse nine. In his capacity as dragon he is pictured as the great devourer. However, what do the heads, horns and crowns represent? Since the language of verse three is similar to verse one, we should expect that the symbols should have a similar meaning in order to be consistent. The woman in the sky cannot be seen, but that which she symbolises, the visible Church, can be seen. Likewise the red dragon will not be seen by the world, but the human organisation which he controls will be seen (compare with Ephesians 6:12; Matthew 12:26). The word of God reveals both sides of the satanic kingdom, the spiritual and the human. The woman symbolises the visible Church, and her crown indicates that the true Church in her will be part of God's heavenly kingdom. The great red dragon symbolises Satan and his demonic kingdom which was and is the real power behind some past human kingdoms and will control the coming world government under Antichrist.

Why is this so? We will examine the symbols in question, and then apply them literally to the vision. These are:

1. **The Great Red Dragon**: The dragon is Satan the devil of verse nine. The colour red symbolises sin (Isaiah 1:18; 63:2). That he is described as being great means there is none like him.

2. **Seven Heads**: Since the symbols of Revelation 12:3 are mentioned again in Revelation 13:1 and 17:3, we can use the angel's explanation in Revelation 17:9-12 to understand their meaning. The seven heads are seven kings, five have been, one was in power when Revelation was written, and one is still to come.

3. **Ten Horns**: The 10 horns represent 10 kings which were still future at the time of writing.

4. **Seven Crowns upon his Heads**: A crown identifies the wearer to be king or prince; it symbolises his authority. Seven is the perfect number. Since Satan is said to be the prince of this world (Ephesians 2:2; John 12:31), the seven crowns would show that he has complete (in the sense of absolute) authority over the coming world government (compare with Luke 4:6-7), and it could symbolise that a total of seven kingdoms form Satan's age-old empire.

If all the symbols are combined with their meaning and put into the vision of verse three, we get Satan the great evil prince who is absolute ruler of this world, ruling over a demonic kingdom which already had six demonic rulers in the past (five plus one principalities Ephesians 6:12). Furthermore his kingdom will have one more ruler (Satan in Antichrist), under which will be 10 lesser kings (demonic powers behind human rulers). Since the red dragon is a contemporary of the woman,

110

the final composition of his kingdom when the 10 kings appear has to be close to the time of the rapture. The demonic side of his kingdom is invisible, just as the woman, but the human side will be seen by the world, just as the visible Church is seen.

To check the accuracy of this interpretation the above symbols and their meaning are applied to the other passages where the same symbols are used, namely Revelation 13:1. If correctly interpreted, there will be harmony between the visions. In Revelation 13:1 there comes a beast out of the sea, having seven heads and 10 horns, and upon his horns 10 crowns, and upon his heads the name of blasphemy. Now these are the same symbols as in the previous vision. But there are two important differences. First, the dragon of chapter 12 appears in the sky, while the beast here comes out of the sea. Second, the dragon has seven crowns upon his heads, while the beast has 10. The first difference shows the two sides of the satanic kingdom. One vision exposes the spiritual side (**he appeared in heaven**), while the other shows the human side of the same kingdom (**the sea symbolises the Gentile nations** Revelation 17:15; Isaiah 17:12-13). The number 10 signifies '**ordinal perfection**' or perfect organisation. Since we now look at the human side of Satan's kingdom, the 10 crowns can indicate that his kingdom is 'perfectly organised'. How fitting when we consider that the coming world government will only be possible because the modern computer makes such an organisation feasible. The 10 crowns also indicate that there will be 10 kingdoms (or nations) which give their authority to Antichrist.

Satan the Great Horn

Revelation 12:4; "*And his tail drew the third part of the stars of heaven, and did cast them to the earth: and the dragon stood before the woman which was ready to be delivered, for to devour her child as soon as it was born.*"

To understand the first part of this verse we must compare it with Daniel 8:10, where the same event is recorded. Daniel reports the exploits of the little horn which became great. The little horn is Antichrist before Satan possesses him. Afterwards when Satan's spirit is in him he becomes great (compare with Revelation 13:2 & 4; Ephesians 6:12). Antichrist will be possessed by Satan's spirit just as Judas was (Luke 22:3). Satan will give Antichrist all his power and authority. But Satan will remain in control. There will be two persons in one body, two in one. That is why when the prophet speaks about Antichrist he sometimes refers to a human person, and sometimes to a spirit. The only way to know to which person in Antichrist the prophet refers is by looking at the context. For example, in Daniel 8:9 the human side is in view, but in the next verse the spiritual.

Daniel 8:10; "*And it waxed great (the little horn Antichrist), to the host of heaven; and it cast down (some) of the host and of the stars to the ground, and stamped upon them.*"

Here Daniel reports the same event as John does in Revelation 12:4. Satan is pictured as the great horn or dragon casting down to earth one third of the host (army) and the stars (angels) of heaven. Why would he do that? And more importantly, how can he do that? One cannot be absolutely certain but the Bible does give some clues by which we can surmise. The following explanation is only a possibility, and should not be taken dogmatically. If you have problems with this, please don't concern yourself further with it.

Satan was Lucifer the anointed cherub, Isaiah 14:12-13; Ezekiel 28:13-14; he had a very high position in the kingdom of God. Yet there came a day when he wanted to have more than was allocated to him, he wanted his own kingdom.

Isaiah 14:12-13; "*How art thou fallen from heaven, O Lucifer, son of the morning! how art thou cut down to the ground, which didst weaken the nations! For thou hast said in thine heart, I will ascend into heaven, I will exalt my throne above the stars of God: I will sit also upon the mount of the congregation, in the side of the north: I will ascend above the heights of the clouds: I will be like the most High.*"

Lucifer was going to exalt himself above the stars (angels) of God. In his ambition he partially succeeded. Somehow he was able to deceive a great number of angels, either to follow him outright, or to believe at least one of his lies. And just one sin is required to make a sinner. Remember Eve. Just one sin brought the whole human race down. Those who followed Satan outright would have been thrown out of heaven immediately. They are the demons (Jude verse 6). However, as in any deception, not everybody is deceived to the same degree. Today in the religious world, some are more deceived than others. Therefore it may be assumed that some angels only believed Satan once, but after that turned away from him. They would have realised the error of their action and no longer followed him. There are two occasions recorded in the Bible which seem to indicate the above.

In 1 Kings 22:21-22, a spirit came and offered himself to serve God in the capacity as a lying spirit. Why would an angel (angels are spirits Hebrews 1:14) of God want to become a lying spirit? The only reason seems to be that by serving God, he hoped he would be forgiven (the salvation by works theory). The other example is in 1 Samuel 16:14-15, where an evil spirit came from God to trouble Saul. Hence there could be spirits in the heavens which are no longer as the holy angels, but do not follow Satan either. Until now Satan for some reason of his own does not force the issue against them. However at a time near the rapture, when the dragon stands before the woman, he will know that his time is almost up. It is then, that he will claim them to be his. And since they have no redeemer, nobody who died for their sin, Satan succeeds in casting them down to earth. He will then stamp on some of them in revenge for not serving him. How grateful Christians can be that Christ Jesus became our Lord and Redeemer. As already mentioned above, this explanation is only a possibility, and should not be taken as dogma.

Why the Dragon wants to Devour the Child

The war which follows the rapture must be the result of the rapture. Why will the war commence at this time? The reason is that the arrival of the saints in heaven spells a major defeat for Satan. Satan has access to heaven, refer to Job 1:6, and Revelation 12:9-10. This privilege is used by him to accuse the saints on earth. He is the accuser of the Christian. God's children are commanded to love God but to hate and abhor evil (Psalm 97:10, Amos 5:15, Romans 12:9). The Christian is exhorted to avoid even the appearance of evil (1 Thessalonians 5:22). Satan is the prince of devils, or evil spirits (Matthew 9:34), consequently what can be more evil than Satan? As such, Christians should not converse with Satan or his evil spirits, also Satan will be bruised under the feet of Christians (Romans 16:20). All this means that the saints and Satan with his demons are eternal enemies (Luke 10:19, 1 Peter 5:8, Ephesians 6:11-12) who cannot be reconciled. Hence it is not possible that Satan and his fallen angels can occupy the same space as the resurrected saints. The Church arrives there ready to fulfil the role which God has allocated for her. Satan who did everything in his power to prevent her from getting there will be thrown out. Even here on earth Satan has to flee from a godly and Spirit filled Christian who resists him (James 4:7). How much more so in heaven after the resurrection. As such it is unimaginable that Christians and Satan could live in the same place and confront each other. The peace and harmony of heaven would be disturbed. God will never allow this to happen.

Therefore when the saints arrive in heaven after the rapture, Satan and those of his angels who are still there will have to go. There is room for only one group. Satan knows this, and for this reason alone he will try anything to prevent the arrival of the saints in heaven.

How the Dragon wants to Devour the Man-Child

The dragon wants to devour the child as soon as it is born. When the Church is raptured, the translated believers may be just as new born babes, and for a while may be disorientated. And so Satan may think that it is at that point that he and his demons have an opportunity to devour the new born child, since the Christians have to travel through his domain, and may appear to be vulnerable before they meet the Lord. This may sound ludicrous. But remember the Devil also tried to destroy the Son of man before he could fend for himself. Satan also attempted to lead Christ into sin. Now if he thought that he could succeed then, would he not try again to devour the child? These are spiritual realms which cannot be fully comprehended today. And of course bearing in mind that whatever happened to the Master will also happen to the servant, (John 15:18-21) therefore if Satan attempted to destroy Jesus Christ when he was a child, will he not try to do the same to the newly translated Church at the time when it appears to be vulnerable? This may be the reason why Michael and his angels will be there to protect the saints, and to wage war on Satan.

What is meant by the expression '*to devour*'? In 1 Peter 5:8, we are told that the devil intends to devour the careless Christian. Obviously this devouring is in the mental or spiritual realm. This devouring consists of deception and/or spiritual blindness which could also lead to fellowship with demons (1 Corinthians 10:20-22). Hence Satan's attempt to devour the 'man-child' must be seen along these lines. Remember Satan knows that when the resurrected saints arrive in heaven he is finished. So he mounts a last desperate attempt to prevent this. His plan could be to deceive the saints with his ability to transform himself as an angel of light. He would appear to the Church as soon as they are translated, and before they meet the Lord. He would hope that Christians would mistaken him for Christ himself since very few would have seen Satan in this deceptive role, and that he could then mislead and devour them. Satan has already succeeded many times in such a role, with people who had near death experiences. These people claim that after they left their body they went through a tunnel. At the other end they were met by a being of brilliant light full of love. Most people claim that this was Jesus Christ himself. However since most of those people were not Christians and saw no need for repentance after their experience, it can be safely assumed that they were deceived by Satan himself. They were met by Satan the angel of light. This could be the desperate plan of Satan to prevent the saints from arriving in heaven. Praise the Lord, we know that Satan's plan is doomed to failure. This explanation is of course only a theory, it may be so or may not be so, but perhaps the true Christians will soon find out.

The Child was 'Caught Up' to God and his Throne

Revelation 12:5; *"And she brought forth a 'man-child', who was to rule all nations with a rod of iron; and her child was caught up unto God, and to his throne."*

The child was '**caught up**' to heaven. A term which indicates the rapture. Note that the child did not '**rise**' to heaven, as did the Lord Jesus. The term '**caught up**' is used in connection with the rapture of the Church and is altogether different to the '**ascension**' of the Lord Jesus.

Why is the child of the woman in Revelation called a '**man-child**' and spoken of as a person, when it symbolises the raptured Church, a body of people? Let us have a look at what has been revealed about it. In Revelation 12:5 we read: *"and she brought forth a **man-child**, who was to rule all nations with a rod of iron: and her child was caught* *up unto God, and to his throne.*" Two things are said about the 'man-child':

1. It is to rule all nations with a rod of iron.

2. It was caught up unto God, and his throne.

Now it is stated in Scripture that both the Lord Jesus and the overcoming believers will rule with a rod of iron, Psalm 2:9 & Revelation 2:27 respectively. Revelation 2:26-27, "*And he that overcometh, and keepeth my works unto the end, to him will I give power over the nations: And he shall rule them with a rod of iron: as the vessels of a potter shall they be broken to shivers: even as I received of my Fathe*r." As far as the above is concerned the '**man-child**' is either the Lord Jesus, or the overcoming believer or perhaps both. Either will fit the condition of the '**man-child**' ruling with a rod of iron. But what about 2. above? The child was caught up to God and to his throne. Where else in Scripture is it said that '**he**' or '**they**' will be caught up to heaven?

1. The Church at the rapture is said to be '**caught up**' together in the air, to be forever with the Lord (1 Thessalonians 4:17).

2. Paul, also a Christian, was said to be '**caught up**' into the third heaven (2 Corinthians 12:2-4).

Therefore the term '**caught up**' is only mentioned in connection with Christians.

But the Lord Jesus at birth was not '**caught up**' to heaven. He remained on earth for about 33 years, and then he ascended slowly, victoriously through the air, the domain of Satan, into heaven. He did not need any assistance, he rose by his own power. But the term '**caught up**' indicates that someone else is providing the power to lift the Church into heaven. Therefore there is a difference between ascending, or being caught up. Only of the Church is it said that she will be '**caught up**'.

Also Revelation 4:1-6 describes a scene in heaven after the Church age. The Church is represented there by the 24 elders who are said to be round about the throne of God. Something else points to the fact that the Church is now in heaven. In Revelation 1:12-13 and 20, the churches are represented by seven lampstands, and of course a lampstand supports a lamp. Note that a lampstand is not the giver of light itself, rather it holds up a lamp, and therefore assists in the spreading of light. In Revelation 4:5 we are informed that seven lamps (**a picture of the complete Holy Spirit**) burn before the throne of God. No lampstand is mentioned. These lamps no longer rest on the lampstand on earth, but have been removed to heaven. All this attests that the Church can no longer function in the spreading of light, and must for this reason have been removed from the earth. The Holy Spirit is said to be in the Christian, and since he has been removed from earth, and is said to be in heaven, the Christians and therefore the Church must likewise be in heaven. The Church is also symbolised by the sea of glass, a picture of the Church out of all Gentile nations. The sea is symbolic for the nations of the world. Compare with Revelation 17:15 and Isaiah 17:12-13. The wicked nations are portrayed as the restless sea whos surface is always in turmoil, just as those nations are always restless and in turmoil. The sea of glass may in contrast represents the saved saints in heaven now completely at ease and rest. All these facts indicate that the Church is in heaven near the throne of God. This would fit the description of the 'man-child' being caught up to the throne of God.

Why is the raptured Church called a 'man-child'? Because the Church is here pictured as the body of Christ.

Romans 12:4-5; *"For as we have many members in one body, and all members have not the same office: So we, being many, are one body in Christ, and every one members one of another."*

1 Corinthians 10:16-17; *"The cup of blessing which we bless, is it not the communion of the blood of Christ? The bread which we break, it is not the communion of the body of Christ: For we [being] many are one bread, and one body: for we are all partakers of that one bread"*

1 Corinthians 12:12-14; *"For as the body is one, and hath many members, and all the members of that one body, being many, are one body: so also is Christ. For by one Spirit are we all baptised into one body, whether we be Jews or Gentiles, whether we be bond or free: and have been all made to drink into one Spirit. For the body is not one member, but many."*

1 Corinthians 12:27; *"Now ye are the body of Christ, and members in particular."*

Ephesians 4:12-16; *"For the perfecting of the saints, for the work of the ministry, for the edifying of the body of Christ: Till we all come in the unity of the faith, and of the knowledge of the Son of God, unto a perfect man, unto the measure of the stature of the fullness of Christ. That we henceforth be no more children, tossed to and fro, and carried about with every wind of doctrine, by the sleight of men, and cunning craftiness, whereby they lie in wait to deceive; But speaking the truth in love, may grow up into him in all things, which is the head, even Christ: From whom the whole body fitly joined together and compacted by that which every joint supplieth, according to the effectual working in the measure of every part, maketh increase of the body unto the edifying of itself in love."*

Ephesians 5:23; *"For the husband is the head of the wife, even as Christ is the head of the church: and he is the saviour of the body."*

Ephesians 5:30; *"For we are members of his body, of his flesh, and of his bones."*

Colossians 1:18; *"And he is the head of the body, the church: who is the beginning, the first-born from the dead; that in all things he might have the pre-eminence."*

Colossians 3:15; *"And let the peace of God rule in your hearts, to the which also ye are called in one body; and be ye thankful."*

Consequently Scripture indicates that the Church is not only the bride and wife of Christ, but also his body, because in the Bible a husband and wife are said to be one flesh (Genesis 2:24). It is this body of Christ which comes forth out of the woman. This body will be perfected, at the time of the rapture. *"And he hath put all under his feet, and gave him the head over all to the church, which is his body, the fullness of him that filleth all in all."* (Ephesians 1:22-23). Therefore *"He will rule with a rod of iron"* can be taken literally, since the 'man-child' (that is the body of Christ) will rule the nations after being caught up to the throne of God.

The Other Man-Child

The symbolism of travailing in birth and bringing forth a 'man-child' is not unique to Revelation 12. In the Old Testament (Isaiah 66:6-8) there is a similar prophecy with a parallel meaning but this time it is the nation Israel which is in view. Just as in Revelation here too the 'man-child' represents a body of people they are the resurrected Old Testament saints. In Revelation the raptured saints, the heavenly people, are fittingly '**brought forth**' by a celestial woman. But the saints of Israel, the earthly covenant people, are '**brought forth**' by the earth.

In the case of both Israel and the Church, the dead shall rise with new bodies, but the living shall be separated into the believing part, and the unbelieving part. The Christians will rise (both dead and living) at the rapture, to go with Christ to heaven. However the nominal Christians who were not raptured will be sent by the Lord into tribulation to prove whether or not they are really prepared to repent. To prove if they love Him more than they love their physical life.

In Israel's case, the graves will be opened and the saved dead (those saved before the Church age) will receive new bodies to live first here on earth during the millennium and thereafter on the new earth and in the new Jerusalem while the unbelieving part will be sent to Hades and later to Hell. The Old Testament saints will be resurrected after the Tribulation and will first inherit all the land of Israel which God promised to them. But they look further than that, to the new Earth and the new Jerusalem, which they together with the Christians will inherit later.

We will now have a look at some Scriptures which confirm the above statements and which refer to Israel's resurrection.

Isaiah. 26:19-21; "*Thy dead men shall live, together with my dead body shall they arise. Awake and sing, ye that dwell in dust; for thy dew is as the dew of herbs, and **the earth shall cast out the dead**. Come, my people, enter thou into thy chambers, and shut thy doors about thee: hide thyself as it were for a little moment, until the indignation be overpast. For, behold, the Lord cometh out of his place to punish the inhabitants of the earth for their iniquity: the earth also shall disclose her blood, and shall no more cover her slain.*"

The prophet Isaiah expects to be raised together with the other godly of Israel. This event will take place after the Tribulation for Israel, when the Lord's indignation against Israel is over and when his fury will be directed against a Christ-rejecting Gentile world, when God will punish the inhabitants of the earth.

Ezekiel 37:11-14; *"Then he said unto me, Son of man, these bones are the whole house of Israel: behold, they say, Our bones are dried, and our hope is lost: we are cut off for our parts. Therefore prophesy and say unto them, Thus saith the Lord God; behold, O my people, I will open your graves, and cause you to come up out of your graves, and bring you into the land of Israel. And ye shall know that I am the Lord, when I have opened your graves, O my people, and brought you up out of your graves. And shall put my spirit in you, and ye shall live, and I shall place you in your own land: then shall ye know that I the Lord have spoken it, and performed it, saith the Lord."*

Once more it is stated that the **graves** will be opened and the people of God will come out of them, to live in the land of Israel. That this happens after Israel's Tribulation is indicated by the statement in verse 14, that God will put his spirit into the children of Israel. That cannot happen during the Tribulation when Israel is still under judgement, but must take place after Israel has repented and acknowledged Jesus Christ as Messiah.

Hosea 13:14; *"I will ransom them from the power of the grave; I will redeem them from death: O death, I will be thy plagues; O grave, I will be thy destruction: repentance shall be hid from mine eyes."*

1 Samuel 2:6; *"The Lord killeth, and maketh alive: he bringeth down to the grave, and bringeth up."*

All the literal earthly promises made to Abraham, Isaac, and Jacob and to their descendants, will be fulfilled to the last jot and tittle (Matthew 5:18) at that time. Everything which was promised to them they will inherit when they will be raised out of the graves. Israel has never yet occupied all the land which is theirs nor have the patriarchs of Israel yet owned the land which was personally given to them (Genesis 13:15-17; 15:18;). But since God's promises will be fulfilled to the last jot and tittle, we must expect that all outstanding promises will be fulfilled during the millennium. To do this God is going to raise out of the grave the godly of Israel and they will literally receive and inherit every outstanding promise. Abraham will finally receive the land which was given to him. However according to Ezekiel 13:9, not all which were of Israel will be part of the future resurrected assembly; not all will inherit the promises.

These Scriptures make it clear that one day the Lord shall open the graves and resurrect his earthly people, that they may enjoy their own land. This opening of the graves does not symbolise the Jews coming out from amongst the Gentile nations. But this will be a literal resurrection of the Jews, who will be raised out from their graves to inherit their land. This is clearly indicated in the above Scriptures and in many others.

This resurrection of Israel's saints is also referred to by Isaiah, in a passage which together with other Scriptures confirms that the 'man-child' is indeed a picture for a group of resurrected saints.

Isaiah 66:5-8; *"Hear the word of the Lord, ye that tremble at his word; Your brethren that hated you, that cast you out for my name's sake, said Let the Lord be glorified: but he shall appear to your joy, and they shall be ashamed. A voice of noise from the city, a voice from the temple, a voice of the Lord that rendereth recompence to his enemies. Before she travailed, she brought forth; before her pain came, she was delivered of a **man-child**. Who hath heard such a thing? who hath seen such a thing? Shall the earth be made to bring forth in one day? or shall a nation be born at once? for as soon as Zion travailed, she brought forth her children."*

Several facts should be noted:

1. A threefold voice is issued forth from the city, from the temple and from the Lord. At the same time the Lord avenges himself of his enemies. As we shall see, when related Scriptures are compared with the one above, this event will happen at the end of Israel's Tribulation, at the start of the day of the Lord. This is indicated by the statement *"he shall appear"*, which refers to the Lord at his second coming, when he will *"render recompense to his enemies"*. This time element is the key to understanding this passage.

2. A 'man-child' comes forth before she (that is the earth) travailed and before her pain came. The earth shall bring forth (out of the graves) a 'man-child' in one day. These are Israel's equivalent to the Church saints who will be raised at the rapture.

3. As soon as Zion travailed she brought forth her (*other*) children. The word '**travailed**' also means '**pain**' and '**grieved**'. All three words imply internal upheaval, they do not refer to external persecution. As such the passage here cannot refer to Israel's time of trouble, but must refer to the painful act of mourning, self-examination, and repentance, after they realised that he whom they have pierced was indeed the very Messiah. This is clearly spelt out in the following Scripture:

Zecharaiah 12:10-14; "*And I will pour upon the house of David, and upon the inhabitants of Jerusalem, the spirit of grace and of supplications: and they shall look upon me whom **they have pierced**, and they shall mourn for him, as one mourneth for [his] only [son], and shall be in bitterness (or grieved) for him, as one that is **in bitterness** for [his] firstborn. In that day shall there be a **great mourning** in Jerusalem, as the mourning of Hadadrimmon in the valley of Megiddon. And the land shall mourn, every family apart; the family of the house of David apart, and their wives apart; the family of the house of Nathan apart, and their wives apart; the family of the house of Levi apart, and their wives apart; the family of Shimei apart, and their wives apart; All the families that remain, every family apart, and their wives apart.*"

The meaning of these verses has already been explained in Part 1 of this Study.

To point 1. above in order to shed more light on this passage we can look at other Scriptures which line up with Isaiah 66:6. The first one is found in Joel:

Joel 3:13-16; "Put ye in the sickle, for the harvest is ripe: come, get you down; for the press is full, the vats overflow; for their wickedness is great. Multitudes, multitudes in the valley of decision: for the day of the Lord is near in the valley of decision. The sun and the moon shall be darkened, and the stars shall withdraw their shining. The

Lord also shall roar out of Zion, and utter his voice from Jerusalem; and the heavens and the earth shall shake: but the Lord will be the hope of his people, and the strength of the children of Israel."

This passage clearly lines up with Isaiah 66, and sheds some more light on the previous text. The context confirms that the time of the fulfilment of both prophecies is the end time which is made clear by the statement that the *"sun and the moon shall be darkened"*. This end time event happens just after the time of Jacob's trouble, but before the Lord returns openly in his glory with his Church (ref. Matthew 24:29). Also in both Scriptures it is stated that the Lord is the hope and the joy of his people. And in Joel clarification is given as to who the originator of the threefold voice of Isaiah 66:6 is. It is the Lord himself.

By combining both verses we are told that at the end time the Lord himself will roar with a threefold voice from Jerusalem and at the same time the heavens and the earth will shake and the Lord will punish his enemies; the day of his indignation has come. But the Lord will be the joy and hope of his people. The time element here is the key to understanding this Scripture.

The same event is mentioned in Isaiah 26:19-21.

"Thy dead men shall live, together with my dead body shall they arise. Awake and sing, ye that dwell in dust: for thy dew is as the dew of herbs, and the earth shall cast out the dead. Come, my people, enter thou into thy chambers, and shut thy doors about thee: hide thyself as it were for a little moment, until the indignation be overpast. For, behold, the Lord cometh out of his place to punish the inhabitants of the earth for their iniquity: the earth also shall disclose her blood, and shall no more cover her slain."

Here too the day of wrath for punishment against the wicked of the world is announced, which shows again that this is an end time event. But something else is written, which clarifies more of Isaiah 66:6. The resurrection of Israel's dead is mentioned. By looking at both Scriptures in conjunction, we begin to understand who the 'man-child' in this context may be. The 'man-child' here represents a body of people, namely the saints of Israel, which will be raised out of their graves. They have been hiding in a place inside the earth until the indignation of God upon the nation of Israel is past. This place is probably the same as "*Abraham's bosom*" to which the Lord referred in Luke 16:22-23. As soon as Israel repents, **the wrath of God is over**, and the saints will be raised. This will become more evident as we look at other Scriptures.

There are two precedents in Scripture where something similar has occurred. When the Lord raised the Jew Lazarus, he shouted with a loud voice and that shout resulted in Lazarus coming forth out of his grave (John 11:43). When the Lord was hanging on the cross, before he gave up his Spirit he shouted "*it is finished*". The earth shook and the graves were opened, and many bodies of the Jewish saints arose (Matthew 27:50-52). Therefore it seems that each resurrection is the direct result of the Lord shouting; He gives the command and the saints rise, and the earth may quake. This is confirmed in 1 Thessalonians 4:16; when the Church is raised, there will also be a threefold voice. The Lord will shout, the archangel will utter his voice and the trump of God will sound. Just as when the saints of Israel are raised here too is a threefold voice.

According to Joel 3:16 the time of the call will be after the time of Jacob's trouble but before the open return of the Lord with his bride. This is made clear by the statement that the sun and the moon will be darkened. This sign is one of the important landmarks in Scripture by which we can pinpoint the time an event takes place. Whenever the context of Scripture refers to the end time, and the darkening of the sun and moon are mentioned, we can instantly connect that passage with Matthew 24:29 and Mark 13:24, where it is clearly stated that this darkening of the sun and moon happens immediately after Israel's Tribulation, but before the open return of the Lord Jesus Christ in Glory with all his saints.

Therefore connecting Isaiah 66:6-8, Joel 3:16 and Isaiah 26:19-21, we learn that after Israel's Tribulation has ended, the sun and moon will be darkened and there will come forth a threefold call from the city of Jerusalem, from the temple on mount Zion, and from the Lord. This will result in the graves being opened, the earth quaking, and the 'man-child' coming forth, which means that the earth is yielding up her dead.

To point 2. above. The 'man-child' comes forth **before** she (*the earth*) travailed and her pain came. The 'she' here refers to the earth which brings forth a people. That the earth is feminine is also shown in Isaiah 26:21; *"The earth shall disclose her blood, and shall no more cover her slain."*

As has already been shown in Isaiah 66, just as in Revelation 12, the 'man-child' represents a body of saved people rising from the dead and being united with the living saints. The only difference here is that the saved belong to Israel and not to the Church. The interpretation of the symbol is consistent, it represents a body of saved people. The differences also are **significant.** The 'man-child' from the woman represents the saints from the Church. They are the heavenly people, and come forth out of a celestial woman. But the 'man-child' representing the saints from Israel, the earthly covenant people, come forth out of the earth. How **significant**. Also in Revelation the child comes forth after the woman is in travail. But in Isaiah the child comes forth before the earth travails. **This fact clearly distinguishes between the two events.**

The Earth in Travail and Pain

The graves will open before the earth shall travail. We have already seen that the threefold call which triggers the opening of the graves will be issued immediately after Israel's Tribulation. By studying the events in that period of time between the end of Israel's Tribulation and the coming of the Lord it becomes evident that the earth will experience upheavals as never before. Many passages which refer to the sun and moon being darkened in the end time also describe terrible upheavals upon the earth. Take for example Luke 21:25-27. The sea will be roaring, men will faint in fear because of the upheavals, the powers of the heavens shall be shaken. The same event is described in Revelation 6:12-15: a great earthquake, stars fall unto the earth, the atmosphere will depart like a scroll rolled together, every mountain and island will be moved out of their place. Consider also the following Scriptures, which show how much the earth will be in pain.

Isaiah 24:1; *"Behold, the Lord maketh the earth empty, and waste, and turneth it upside down, and scattereth abroad the inhabitants thereof."*

Isaiah 24:19-20; *"The earth is utterly broken down, the earth is clean dissolved, the earth is moved exceedingly. The earth shall reel to and fro like a drunkard, and shall be removed like a cottage; and the transgression thereof shall be heavy upon it; and it shall fall, and not rise again."*

The reason for the troubles upon the earth are the transgressions of the people. The Lord will punish the inhabitants of the world by causing upheavals in the earth. Surely the earth will travail and be in pain, after the 'man-child' has come out of her. The earth will bring forth the saints of Israel in one day, but after that there will be pain and travail for the earth and for the Gentiles. But Israel will not have to fear, because they have the Lord who protects them. (Joel 3:16). As such it is evident that the 'man-child' in the Old as well as in the New Testament represents a body of saved people. This interpretation seems consistent and fits both prophecies in every respect. No far-fetched symbols have to be employed in an effort to make the passage fit the interpretation.

One more point to confirm is that in most cases a literal interpretation of the Old Testament passages is warranted. Not only will the Lord open the graves to raise the saints of Israel, but King David will literally be reinstated as King over them.

Jeremiah 30:7-10; *"Alas! for that day is great, so that none is like it: it is even the time of Jacob's trouble; but he shall be saved out of it. For it shall come to pass in that day, saith the Lord of hosts, that I will break his yoke from off thy neck, and will burst thy bonds, and strangers shall no more serve themselves of him: But they shall serve the Lord their God, and David their King, whom I will raise up unto them. Therefore fear thou not, O my servant Jacob, saith the Lord; neither be dismayed, O Israel: for, lo, I will save thee from afar, and thy seed from the land of their captivity; and Jacob shall return, and shall be in rest, and be quiet, and none shall make him afraid."*

Here it is written that David will be raised again to be the King of Israel. Also living Israel will be gathered from all over the world, and they will live in peace in their own land.

Ezekiel 34:23-25; *"And I will set up one shepherd over them, and he shall feed them, even my servant David; he shall feed them, and he shall be their shepherd. And I the Lord will be their God, and my servant David a prince among them; I the Lord have spoken it. And I will make with them a covenant of peace, and will cause the evil beasts to cease out of the land: and they shall dwell safely in the wilderness, and sleep in the woods."*

The Scriptures show that David will be raised to be leader of the new nation of Israel. The Lord has spoken and there should be no more discussions about this fact.

Ezekiel 37:24-28; *"And David my servant shall be King over them; and they all shall have one shepherd: they shall also walk in my judgements, and observe my statutes, and do them. And they shall dwell in the land that I have given unto Jacob my servant, wherein your fathers have dwelt; and they shall dwell therein, even they, and their children, and their children's children forever: and my servant David shall be their prince forever. Moreover I will make a covenant of peace with them: it shall be an everlasting covenant with them: and I will place them, and multiply them, and will set my sanctuary in the midst of them for evermore. My tabernacle also shall be with them: yea, I will be their God, and they shall be my people. And the heathen shall know that I the Lord do sanctify Israel, when my sanctuary shall be in the midst of them for evermore."*

Hosea 3:4-5; *"For the children of Israel shall abide many days without a King, and without a Prince, and without a sacrifice, and without an image, and without an ephod, and without teraphim. Afterward shall the children of Israel return, and seek the Lord their God, and David their King; and shall fear the Lord and his goodness in the latter days."*

We now to return to the 'man-child' brought forth by the woman of Revelation chapter 12.

The Woman in the Wilderness

Revelation 12:6, & 13-14, "*And the woman fled into the wilderness, where she hath a place prepared of God, that they should feed her there a thousand two hundred and threescore days..... And when the dragon saw that he was cast unto the earth, he persecuted the woman which brought forth the **man-child**. And to the woman were given two wings of a great eagle, that she might fly into the wilderness, into her place, where she is nourished for a time and times, and half a time, from the face of the serpent.*"

After the birth of the 'man-child' the woman has lost her prominent position in the sky and she is no longer clothed with the sun, nor has she the moon under her feet. Her power and glory were in the child (*the true believers, the body of Christ*). Once they are gone, the Holy Spirit is gone from her, and she finds herself powerless. Even the name '**visible Church**' should no longer be used, but the term of Revelation chapter 12 '**the woman**' would be the better description from now on. Because those left are no longer part of the Church, they are the '**remnant of her seed**'.

Those who are left are the nominal deceived Christians and hypocrites. They are no match for the forces of darkness and therefore have to run for their life. At this time Satan can persecute the woman without the Holy Spirit restraining him. The woman has to flee into a wilderness to a place which God has prepared for her. Hence the remnant *(those who were deceived)* will flee to a location somewhere on earth which God even now is preparing for them. There the woman will be safe for a while. This place may be a country which had a Christian government. This country may welcome the remnant, especially if they manage to bring some of the woman's former massive wealth with them. The remaining part which belonged to the visible Church, now stripped not only of the true believers (*at the rapture*), but also of many of her nominal believers, will consist mainly of the wicked and apostates. They will unite into the Babylonian harlot of Revelation 17 and are no longer part of the woman.

After the dragon is cast out of heaven he directs his fury and his anger against the remnant of the woman. He did not succeed in preventing the rapture of the saints, and so those which loved their old self-life more than the Lord Jesus and had never truly repented, now have to pay for his defeat. The restrainer (2 Thessalonians 2:6-8) no longer hinders Satan in his persecution against the woman.

However, God's redemptive plan stands fast, and can never be defeated by Satan. All his persecution of the professing Christian does is to turn many in true repentance to Jesus Christ. Many of those in leadership and multitudes of others (*only those which were deceived*), finally have their eyes opened and repent of their old carnal ways. They decide to gather somewhere on earth, where God has a place prepared. According to verse 6 **they** probably refers to the people who live in or near that place. They will feed the woman for 3½ years. Verse 17 tells us that the dragon makes war against the remnant of the woman's seed. A war means action and fighting from both sides, so we can assume that the remnant will be engaged in aggressive evangelisation. However as we shall see, Satan will overcome the woman. The time segment of 3½ years gives us a clue by which we can identify other Scriptures dealing with the same subject.

The Prophet Daniel was living amongst the Gentiles. His prophecies concern both Jew and Gentile. Which group he wrote about has to be determined by the context of each passage. For instance Daniel 7:22-28 speaks about the saints of the Most High, a term which fits the Tribulation saints. It cannot refer to Israel. They would not be called 'saints of the most high' before they have repented. And after they have repented Antichrist will certainly not be able to wear them out, nor is it likely that he will be around for another 3½ years after Israel has been purified. Since that passage lines up with Revelation chapters 12 and 13 it is reasonably certain that the passage in Daniel applies to the remnant of the Church. By studying the **'Scripture Comparison Chart'** on page 131, we notice that Antichrist (the horn) wages war against the remnant and wins. It is a drawn out war because it rages for 3½ years, but the revived believers cannot win without the restraining power of the Holy Spirit. Those of the remaining believers who are overcome are killed, and we find them again in heaven (Revelation 6:9-11). They ask for revenge, but the 3½ years are not yet up, the last believer has not yet arrived in heaven, and therefore they have to wait a little longer. We can also read that Antichrist will blaspheme against God and those that dwell in heaven. Those that dwell in heaven would refer to the raptured saints, none of which Satan could prevent from getting there. Therefore he slanders and insults them. But the judgement shall sit and from that point on, the power of Antichrist will decline, his power and kingdom will be consumed and destroyed, then when the Lord finally returns in glory he will be finished altogether. It could be that the judgement against Antichrist's authority will be conducted in heaven from the throne of Christ in conjunction with the 24 elders (ministers) of his government, as is indicated in Revelation 4:1-5.

At what time the woman will flee into the wilderness is difficult to determine, but it would have to be after the rapture and before the end of the Gentile tribulation. The 3½ years of war between the woman and Satan could, but does not have to, run parallel with Israel's Tribulation, since they are two independent events.

Chart No 4
Scripture Comparison Chart

Daniel Ch 7	Rev Ch 12	Rev Ch 13
V21. I beheld, and the same horn made war with the saints, and prevailed against them. V25. And he shall speak great words against the most High, and shall wear out the saints of the most High, and think to change times and laws: and they shall be given into his hand until a time and times and the dividing of time. (3½ years) V26. But the judgment shall sit, and they shall take away his dominion, to consume and to destroy it unto the end.	V13. And when the dragon saw that he was cast unto the earth, he persecuted the woman which brought forth the 'man-child' V14. And to the woman was given two wings of a great eagle, that she might fly into the wilderness, into her place, where she is nourished for a time, and times, and a half a time, from the face of the serpent. (3½ years) V17. And the dragon was wroth with the woman, and went to make war with the remnant of her seed, which keep the commandments of God, and have the testimony of Jesus Christ.	V5. And there was given unto him a mouth speaking great things and blasphemies; and power was given unto him to continue forty and two months (3½ years) V6. And he opened his mouth in blasphemy against God, to blaspheme his name, and his tabernacle, and them that dwell in heaven. V7. And it was given unto him to make war with the saints, and to overcome them: and power was given him over all kindreds, and tongues, and nations.

War in Heaven

Revelation 12:7-9; "*And there was war in heaven: Michael and his angels fought against the dragon; and the dragon fought and his angels, and prevailed not; neither was their place found anymore in heaven. And the great dragon was cast out, that old serpent, called the Devil, and Satan, which deceiveth the whole world: he was cast out into* (better 'to') *the earth, and his angels were cast out with him.*"

The scene returns to the end of verse five, after Satan's attempt to devour the 'man-child'. The reason why Satan wants to devour the child has already been addressed. To prevent this from happening Michael and his angels stand ready for action.

The question could arise, why are the angels required to protect the resurrected saints? Surely, the Lord Jesus himself would be more than able to protect his bride. Yes, but it is part of the ministry of angels to help Christians (Hebrews 1:14). Secondly there may be a principle involved here. Satan and his host are fallen angels. As such they tarnished the reputation of the whole angelic race. In order to cleanse their name, God may give his holy angels an opportunity to throw the rebels out themselves. Also, as was shown while investigating verse four, there must be some angels in heaven who sinned only once. Nevertheless, because of this they still belonged to Satan. If this thought is taken a step further, then it would follow that there must be a borderline. Some angels did indeed sin, yet others may have only been tempted yet never actually went through with it. The war in heaven may also involve a claim of Satan against these angels. By being allowed to fight against the satanic host, God shows to all that these angels belong to him and not to Satan.

There is another question. In 1 Thessalonians 4:16 we are informed that at the time of the rapture, the Lord will descend from heaven with a shout, with the voice of the archangel and with the trump of God. What is the significance of this?

By looking at the Thessalonian passage and comparing it with Revelation 12:7 we seem to have the answer. The Lord Jesus himself descends to bring home his bride. He shouts to raise the dead and to translate the living saints. The archangel must be Michael, since Jude verse 9 informs us that he is an archangel. Also we know that Michael will stand up for Israel at the time of their great Tribulation to help them (Daniel 12:1). Therefore a part of Michael's ministry is to wage war against satanic forces in order to help the people of God. This seems to be the case for the Christians during the Church age, and for the Jews after the Church age. Therefore the voice of the archangel is heard to give instructions to his angelic host. The trump of God will sound to start the action.

Satan and his host will be thrown out of heaven to make way for the translated Church. This must be the event the Lord Jesus foresaw in Luke 10:18 when he saw Satan as lightning fall from heaven.

Where in heaven will this war take place? The Greek word for heaven 'ouranos' can mean both sky or space, or heaven the abode of God. We must therefore determine by content which place is in view, in any particular Scripture.

As has already been shown, the position of the woman had to be in the sky. But where is the actual war fought? Revelation 12:12 seems to provide at least a clue. *"Therefore rejoice, ye heavens, and ye that dwell in them."* Here is indicated that there exists more than one heaven, and that these heavens have inhabitants. In Nehemiah 9:6 there is a further indication that there may be more than one heaven. *"Thou hast made heaven, the heaven of heavens, with all their host,"* If we take this literally, then it would mean that there exists a heaven which is above other heavens. But the other heavens have creatures living in them.

2 Chronicles 18:18; *"Again he said, Therefore hear the word of the LORD; I saw the LORD sitting upon his throne, and all the host of heaven standing on his right hand and [on] his left."*

Here it is stated that the host of heaven stands in the presence of God, which shows us that in some instances the expression 'the host of heaven' refers to beings.

Ephesians 3:10; *"To the intent that now unto the principalities and powers in heavenly places might be known by the church the manifold wisdom of God."*

Those in heavenly places can learn of God's wisdom when they observe how he deals with the Church. A further passage which sheds light on this subject is Job 1:7;

"And the Lord said unto Satan, Whence comest thou? Then Satan answered the Lord, and said, from going to and fro in the earth, and from walking up and down in it."

God's question was obviously asked for our benefit, and for the benefit of the sons of God which were present, since God knew full well where Satan had come from. But there is an interesting implication. If Satan had access to only the earth and the heaven where that assembly had gathered, then his answer would have been meaningless. Of course he had to come from earth, if that was his only permitted place of abode. But if there are other places, like other planets or galaxies where he could have been, then his answer makes sense. If the sons of God had also come from these other places, then they had no way of knowing where Satan may have been. Therefore God had to ask that question.

This could indicate (but one can't be sure), that the expression in Revelation 12:12 *"ye heavens, and ye that dwell in them."* may refer to other planets or galaxies. If that is the case, then it may be from there that Satan and his host are evicted. But regardless where the war takes place, Satan himself has access to God, because he accuses us before him day and night.

How long the war in heaven will last we are not told. It may be short, or it could last a while. The duration of this war would be a factor in determining at what time the woman would flee into the wilderness. Also the time between the start of Satan's persecution and the woman deciding to flee is not known. Both of these unknown factors prevent us from knowing the beginning of the 3½ years which the woman will spend in the wilderness. Nowhere is it stated that these 3½ years which the woman spends in the wilderness have to coincide with the beginning or the middle of Israel's Tribulation. Both events are independent of each other.

Revelation 12:10; *"And I heard a loud voice saying in heaven, Now is come salvation, and strength, and the kingdom of our God, and the power of his Christ: for the accuser of our brethren is cast down, which accuses them before God day and night."*

After Satan is cast out, there is rejoicing in heaven, because the accuser of the brethren is cast out. Several facts are mentioned:

1. It must be a Christian whose loud voice is heard in heaven, because he calls those which overcame Satan by the blood of the Lamb, his brethren.

2. He states that only now is come salvation (the consummation of salvation), and strength and God's kingdom and the power of Christ.

3. The reason for this new state of affairs is that Satan the accuser has been cast down.

4. Satan has accused the brethren of this Christian day and night before God.

Those who are accused by Satan must be Christians. They overcame him by the blood of the Lamb. Only Christians can do that. Therefore the speaker in verse 10 must likewise be a Christian. He must be a saint who has been in the presence of the Lord in his spirit for a considerable length of time. Because to be absent from the body is to be present with the Lord (2 Corinthians 5:8), he, and others like him, would have observed throughout the centuries how Satan comes to bring his accusations against the Christians on earth before God. Those charges must have had some effect, since full salvation and strength could not be given to the Church as long as Satan could act in this manner. There must be a legal ground which prevents the Church from exercising her full authority, for as long as Satan can bring accusations against her.

The case may be similar to an earthly court case. As long as new charges are brought against an accused which have to be considered, the accused has his rights curtailed. Only after the case has been dismissed and the accused is declared innocent, can his full rights be restored. This may be the case between the Church and Satan. The consummation of salvation and with it full strength and the kingdom of God cannot come so long as Satan is allowed to bring fresh charges against Christians before God for consideration. Perhaps it is for this reason that Satan does not cease to bring new ones against us day and night, to draw out his case as long as possible.

Revelation 12:11; *"And they overcame him by the blood of the Lamb, and by the word of their testimony; and they loved not their lives unto the death."*

Those who overcame Satan are the brethren (Christians) of the speaker in verse 10. Christians here on earth (if they indeed are Christians) are overcomers. The act of overcoming has to be performed here on earth. We are not aware when Satan accuses us. Nevertheless since we know that Satan has many occasions in our lives where he could accuse us, we should understand that he lets no opportunity go by without doing so. But we can overcome all his accusations by claiming the cleansing power of the blood of the Lamb, and by confessing before men that Christ Jesus is indeed Lord, God and Saviour. This is plain Christian doctrine and easy to understand. However, what is meant by the expression *"they loved not their lives unto death."*?

The implication is that none of those who arrived in heaven loved their life. It appears that all those who had been raptured or resurrected hated their life. Now please note that not all of them who had arrived in heaven would have been killed for their faith here on earth. Therefore the statement that they loved not their lives unto death can have no reference to the physical life of those who had arrived in heaven. The life in question here must be the old nature, the old self, the law of sin in our flesh, the old Adamic self-life, which every human inherits at birth.

In Luke 14:26-27 we read:

"If any man come to me, and hate not his father, his mother, and wife, and children, and brethren, and sisters, yea, and his own life also, he cannot be my disciple. And whosoever doth not bear his cross, and come after me, cannot be my disciple."

Obviously, the Lord did not mean that we hate our loved ones in the same sense that the world understands hate. But we are to hate the old nature, the **old selfish me**, which is in our loved ones, yes and of course in us. This old self-life did not originate from God, but from Satan. At the very moment when Adam and Eve sinned, they died to the spiritual life which was in them and they exchanged it for a selfish nature - the same nature that Satan has. This is why the Lord could say to the Jews in John 8:44; *"Ye are of your father the devil, and the lusts* *of your father ye will do.*" Satan together with all natural men will always act to satisfy their own lusts. The self-life demands it, and it will always strive to be satisfied.

The Lord also said in Luke 14:27; *"whosoever doth not bear his cross, and come after me, cannot be my disciple"*. Now he that carries a cross is on the way to his execution. That is the only purpose of a cross. Likewise every Christian should be on his way to have his old nature executed. This principle is further enlarged in John 12:25, *"He that loveth his life shall lose it; and he that hateth his life in this world shall keep it unto life eternal."* He who loves his old self-life, which is full of envy, lust, pride, and temper etc. will lose it if he does not repent and he will end up in hell. But he that hates this life inside of him which he has in this world, shall receive a new life, at the time of his new birth. This new life he will keep for eternity.

Consequently those Christians who had been resurrected or raptured according to Revelation 12:11 seem to have hated their old selfish life, even to the point where they wanted it to die. Paul the Apostle hated that old nature, that law of sin in his flesh. In Romans 7:13-25 he informs us about the battle he had. Paul calls it *"the law of sin which is in my members,"* verse 23. Paul did not love that old life of his, and wanted it to die, verse 24. He did that which every Christian should do, he committed the problem to his Lord, and the Lord indeed dealt with that sin in Paul's flesh. Paul died to that old self-nature in his flesh. In Philippians 4:9-13 we read about a different Paul, a victorious Paul who was content in every way. But the important fact is that first of all Paul had a desire to die to self.

Every Christian who is truly converted should have the desire to die to self. With some people it may be stronger than with others, but no Christian should love that old sin life in his flesh. Those who **claim** to be Christians and yet enjoy feeding the old nature, may wake up with a shock when they are left behind at the rapture and are confronted by the Antichrist.

Revelation 12:12; *"Therefore rejoice, ye heavens, and ye that dwell in them. Woe to the inhabitants of the earth and of the sea! for the devil is come down unto you, having great wrath, because he knoweth that he hath but a short time."*

After the removal of Satan and his angels, the inhabitants of the heavens (galaxies?) are exhorted to rejoice, since at that time a new ruling class has arrived, and is ready to take its place in the government of God. But woe to those still living on the earth.

Revelation 12:15-16; "*And the serpent cast out of his mouth water as a flood after the woman, that he might cause her to be carried away of the flood. And the earth helped the woman, and the earth opened her mouth, and swallowed up the flood which the dragon cast out of his mouth.*"

The Greek word for cast is '*ballo*', meaning to throw violently, or intensively. The implication here is that Satan throws up water after the woman. His hate is intense, and he wants the destruction of those who claim the Lord Jesus as Lord and Saviour. Satan will be using the big mouth of Antichrist (Revelation 5-6) to cast out hate like a flood of water after the woman. This in turn will cause a multitude of people to go after her. In Jeremiah 47:1-3 an invading army is pictured as an overflowing flood. Likewise in Psalm 124:1-5 it is stated that men rose up against Israel like water to overwhelm them. And in Isaiah 17:12-13 the multitude of many people is compared to the rushing of many waters. Hence the symbolism of this verse implies that, motivated by the hate which Satan spits out using the mouth of Antichrist, a multitude of people will like a flood follow the woman, trying to destroy her.

A mild preview of what will happen can already be observed today. The establishment media, in conjunction with some pseudo-Christian publications have elevated themselves to be judge and guardian of society. Anybody who disagrees with them, and especially those with an earnest desire to serve the Lord Jesus uncompromisingly in spirit and in truth, are labelled crackpot fanatics. They are portrayed as unstable lunatics with a machine gun in the right hand and the Bible in the left hand, who should be locked up. The media, and the so-called experts on the cults band together to denounce anybody who will not fit in with their idea of Christianity. This is happening today while the restrainer is still operative. How much worse will it be after Satan is cast out of heaven?

The earth will help the woman by swallowing up the flood. The natural disasters that will happen after the rapture will neutralise much of the armies following after the woman. There will be tidal waves, massive earthquakes, volcanic eruptions on a scale never seen before. All will help the woman to avoid total annihilation for a time.

Satan and his Host

Who is the host of the high ones, who, according to Isaiah 24:21-22, will be shut up in prison? Who are the sons of God, or the angels which kept not their first estate? (Jude verse 6). Let us now continue this Study by looking at related Scriptures to find the answer, because to find the answers to these questions is important in our study of Revelation chapter 12.

Nehemiah 9:6; *"Thou, [even] thou, [art] LORD alone; thou hast made heaven, the heaven of heavens, with all their host, the earth and all [things] that [are] therein, the seas, and all that [is] therein, and thou preservest them all; and the **host of heaven worshippeth** thee."*

Only living beings can worship. Therefore the host of heaven in the above verse must refer to intelligent creatures.

Luke 2:13-14; *"And suddenly there was with the angel a multitude of the heavenly host praising God, and saying, Glory to God in the highest, and on earth peace, good will toward men."*

The context here shows that the heavenly host mentioned in this verse arc angels.

1 Kings 22:19; *"And he said, Hear thou therefore the word of the LORD: I saw the LORD sitting on his throne, and all the host of heaven standing by him on his right hand and on his left."* (Compare with 2 Chronicles 18:18).

The host of heaven has access to God.

Psalm 148:2; *"Praise ye him, all his angels: praise ye him, all his hosts."*

Note: The heavenly host consists of angels.

Job 1:6; "*Now there was a day when the sons of God came to present themselves before the LORD, and Satan came also among them.*" (Compare with Job 2:1).

The sons of God are beings who are directly created by God. The angels are sons of God. Satan is a son of God, alas, a fallen one. Adam was a son of God. Every born again Christian is a new creature (2 Corinthians 5:17), and therefore a son of God. (1 John 3:1).

Job 38:4 & 7; "*Where wast thou when I laid the foundations of the earth? ... When the morning starts sang together, and all the sons of God shouted for joy?*"

The angels (the sons of God) were already there when God created the earth.

2 Kings 17:16; "*And they left all the commandments of the LORD their God, and made them molten images, [even] two calves, and made a grove, and worshipped all the host of heaven, and served Baal.*"

Humans can fall into the trap of worshipping the host of heaven, which in this case are fallen angels.

2 Chronicles 33:3; "*For he built again the high places which Hezekiah his father has broken down, and he reared up altars for Baalim, and made groves, and **worshipped** all the host of heaven, **and served them.***"

Some humans not only worship the host of heaven, but actually serve them. This shows again that some of the host of heaven are beings who crave men's worship, and must therefore be fallen angels.

Jeremiah 19:13; "*And the houses of Jerusalem, and the houses of the kings of Judah, shall be defiled as the place of Tophet, because of all ... houses upon whose roofs they have burned incense unto all the ... heaven, and have poured out drink offerings unto **other gods**.*"

... angels love to be worshipped as gods. To be like God was ... on and caused his fall.

Job 4:18; *"Behold, he put no trust in his servants; and his angels he charged with folly."*

The word folly means error. The fallen angels committed an error which had terrible consequences.

Genesis 6:2; *"That the sons of God saw that daughters of men that they [were] fair; and they took them wives of all which they chose."*

Here we are told that the sons of God (fallen angels) desired human women.

Genesis 6:4; *"There were giants in the earth in those days; and also after that, when the sons of God came in unto the daughters of men, and they bare [children] to them, the same [became] mighty men which [were] of old, men of renown."*

The fallen angels were able to have intercourse with human women. This resulted in the birth of children and was a grave error.

Matthew 25:41; *"Then shall he say also unto them on the left hand, Depart from me, ye cursed, into everlasting fire, prepared for the devil and his angels."*

The devil and his angels will be sent to hell, which was especially created for them, but of course, also for those who follow him.

Jude Verse 6; *"And the angels which kept not their first estate, but left their own habitation, he hath reserved in everlasting chains under darkness unto the judgment of the great day."*

2 Peter 2:4; *"For if God spared not the angels that sinned, but cast [them] down to hell, and delivered [them] into chains of darkness, to be reserved unto judgment;"*

Those of the fallen angels which stepped out of their line and used human women are already confined to the pit.

1 Corinthians 6:3; *"Know ye not that we shall judge* (or govern) *angels? How much more things that pertain to this life."*

The rest of the angels who are still at liberty will be judged by Christians (that is if the text here refers to fallen angels). But if the text refers to the holy angels, then Christians would govern them, as mentioned before.

Daniel 8:10; "*And it waxed great [even] to the host of heaven; and it cast down [some] of the host and of the stars to the ground, and stamped upon them.*"

Sometimes '**stars**' refer to Satan's host, or is a name for a servant of God. At other times a literal star is in view. In the verse above the host of heaven are fallen angels who are probably punished by Satan for disobedience.

After Satan magnified himself and wanted to be like the most High, God told him what he would do. Satan would be progressively, in seven steps, brought down to nothing.

Ezekiel 28:14-19; "*Thou [art] the anointed cherub that covereth; and I have set thee [so]: thou wast upon the holy mountain of God; thou hast walked up and down in the midst of the stones of fire. Thou [wast] perfect in thy ways from the day that thou wast created, till iniquity was found in thee. By the multitude of thy merchandise they have filled the midst of thee with violence, and thou hast sinned: therefore I will cast thee as profane out of the mountain of God: and I will destroy thee, O covering cherub, from the midst of the stones of fire. Thine heart was lifted up because of thy beauty, thou hast corrupted thy wisdom by reason of thy brightness: I will cast thee to the ground, I will lay thee before kings, that they may behold thee. Thou hast defiled thy sanctuaries by the multitude of thine iniquities, by the iniquity of thy traffic; therefore will I bring forth a fire from the midst of thee, it shall devour thee, and I will bring thee to ashes upon the earth in the sight of all them that behold thee. All they that know thee among the people shall be astonished at thee: thou shalt be a terror, and never [shalt] thou [be] any more.*"

The first three downward progressions in the career of Satan have already been accomplished. He has been cast out of God's mountain (God's government), his powerful position has been destroyed, and the guardian cherub drove him out from the brilliant place in which he lived.

Ezekiel 28:16; (RSV 1973 National Council of Churches of Christ) "*In the abundance of your trade you were filled with violence, and you sinned; so I cast you as a profane thing from the mountain of God, and the guardian cherub drove you out from the midst of the stones of fire.*"

The next four downward steps are sure to follow, we can find out more about this in the following Scriptures:

Revelation 12:7-9; "*And there was war in heaven: Michael and his angels fought against the dragon; and the dragon fought and his angels, And prevailed not; neither was there place found any more in heaven. And the great dragon was cast out, that old serpent, called the Devil, and Satan, which deceiveth the whole world: he was cast out into (*down to*) the earth, and his angels were cast out with him.*"

Revelation 12:12; "*Therefore rejoice, [ye] heavens, and **ye that dwell in them**. Woe to the inhabiters of the earth and of the sea! for the devil is come down unto you, having great wrath, because **he knoweth that he hath but a short time**.*"

Here the fourth descent of Satan is foretold. He and his host will be thrown out of heaven down to earth, and later after a short time, at the end of the day of the Lord, they will be shut up in the pit as is predicted in the verses below (compare also with Revelation 20:2-3). Also note that there will be a twofold cleansing. First the heavens will be cleansed from all of Satan's host. They are cast unto the earth as is shown above. After that the land of Israel will be cleansed from all unclean spirits, that is Satan's host on earth. (Refer to Zechariah 13:2). One more point, after the heavens (other galaxies?) have been cleansed from the satanic host, those which dwell in them are admonished to rejoice, which means that other beings must occupy those heavenly places.

Isaiah 24:21-22; "*And it shall come to pass in that day, [that] the LORD shall punish the **host of the high ones** [that are] on high, and the kings of the earth upon the earth. And they shall be gathered together, [as] prisoners are gathered in the pit, and shall be shut up in the prison, and **after many days** shall they be visited.*"

The same event is under consideration. But note that the kings from the earth are also gathered at the same time. They also will be shut up with the satanic host in the pit. This is the time when Satan will lay before kings, as is written in Ezekiel 28:17. This would be his fifth demotion.

Isaiah 34:3-5; "*Their slain also shall be cast out, and their stink shall come up out of their carcases, and the mountains shall be melted with their blood. And all the host of heaven shall be dissolved (*pine away*), and the heavens shall be rolled together as a scroll: and all their host shall fall down, as the leaf falleth off from the vine, and* **as a falling [fig] from the fig tree.** *For my sword shall be bathed in heaven: behold, it shall come down upon Idumea, and upon the people of my curse, to judgment.*"

These two passages in Isaiah 34 and Revelation 6 below are parallel. They describe events which start with the war in heaven and will climax during the day of the Lord. The stars in the passage below can mean either an angel (in this case fallen ones), or a meteorite, or both. The passage above must include Satan's host in its reference to fallen stars, since no meteorite could be falling to earth as slowly as a leaf. These two verses describe the two aspects of that time. It informs us what takes place in heaven and what, as a partial consequence of that, will happen on earth.

Revelation 6:12-17; "*And I beheld when he had opened the sixth seal, and, lo, there was a great earthquake; and the sun became black as sackcloth of hair, and the moon became as blood; And the stars of heaven fell unto the earth, even as a* **fig tree casteth her untimely figs**, *when she is shaken of a mighty wind. And the heaven departed as a scroll when it is rolled together; and every mountain and island were moved out of their places. ... And said to the mountains and rocks, fall on us, and hide us from the face of him that sitteth on the throne, and from the wrath of the Lamb: for the great day of his wrath is come; and who shall be able to stand*:?

This passage makes known to us what transpires on earth while the war in heaven is fought. The host of heaven shall pine away. Luther translated the expression 'the host of heaven' as 'the army of heaven'. It is this army of Satan that will pine away. They will be defeated in one skirmish after another. This war will not be a 'Blitz Krieg', but will take some time. Michael and his angels will search out the rebels in the heavens and in a series of battles will defeat them and dissolve that army. Some of Satan's host will be falling down to earth like leaves from the vine; that is slowly but steadily, one after the other. Therefore it is possible that the war in heaven starts soon after the rapture, and probably lasts until the day of the Lord - that is, after the time of Jacob's trouble. However, Satan himself could be the first who is thrown out. While all this takes place in the heavens the day of the Lord, with all of its upheavals, is ushered in on earth. At this stage more than Satan's angels will fall to the earth. Literal meteorites will, like ripe figs, smash into the earth.

Satan's sixth and seventh demotions most likely take place after the millennium, after he has led the last human rebellion against God. It is then that fire from God will consume everything. (Compare Revelation 20:9).

The Woman had other Children

Revelation 12:17; *"And the dragon was wroth with the woman, and went to make war with the remnant of her seed, which kept the commandments of God, and have the testimony of Jesus Christ."*

The woman has some other seed, '**he remnant**'. These are those who had never truly repented and been born again from above. They had been deceived, having been led to believe that they were Christians. They were made to believe that they were Christians purely because they had one day made a mental decision for Christ. But they will still have the opportunity to come to a saving knowledge of Christ after the rapture, during the tribulation for the Gentiles, as already discussed. They will in all probability be killed for their faith. The 'other seed' of the woman must also, like the 'man-child', be of the same kind as the woman. They too must represent a body of people. They will become brothers and sisters of the 'man-child'.

The other seed are those people who today think they are saved but have never truly **repented**. They would include people from every denomination including Roman Catholics, members of apostate Protestantism and misguided Pentecostals etc. These people were never told the true meaning of repentance. They were told that to merely accept Christ or to have the sacraments ministered to them was all that was required. They never understood the true meaning of a **new birth**, as the word of God demands. Nor the meaning of true repentance or the need to hate and perhaps die to the old self- life, inherited from Adam. As such they were left in the belief that they were Christians, when in reality a true regeneration in their lives had never taken place. Many of them will only understand when they realise that they have been left behind at the rapture and when they see the Antichrist rising to power during the Tribulation.

This lines up with Revelation 2:22-23 where the children of Thyatira (Roman Catholic) are said to be cast into great tribulation, where they will be killed. It is sad to know that multitudes of sincere people work and give much for their 'church', believing that by these acts they will work their way to heaven; alas, all are not born again. How important it is to trust the Lord Jesus Christ and him alone. But as has already been said, many of those who are left behind will repent when persecution comes.

Here is proof again that the remnant of the woman's seed will be believers in Christ. They keep the commandments of God and testify for Jesus Christ; only those who belong to Christ do that. If Israel represented the woman, they would have to testify for Christ immediately after the rapture, but we know from Daniel 9:24 that the reconciliation for their iniquity will only be made **after** the 70 weeks have run their course. The very Tribulation will be used by God to lead them to Christ. As such they cannot testify at the beginning of the Tribulation. Therefore here it is shown again, that the woman of Revelation chapter 12 can't be Israel.

Israel in the Wilderness - A type of the Woman

There seems to be a principle in the Bible that what happened, or what was promised to Israel, often finds its fulfilment in Jesus Christ or the Church. Especially in the spiritual realm. Take as one example the bread coming down from heaven to sustain Israel's physical life (Exodus 16:4). In John 6:48-58, the Lord Jesus spoke about himself being the

Chart No 5 - All of Israel compared with the Woman in Heaven

Israel	The Woman
Israel, an assembly of God's people. Acts 7:38	The visible Church, an assembly of God's people
For they are not all Israel, which are of Israel. Romans 9:6	Not everyone that saith unto me, Lord, Lord, shall enter into the kingdom of heaven. Matthew 7:21-23
Israel: Ye shall be a peculiar treasure unto me above all people. Exodus 19:5	**The Church:** But ye are a chosen generation, ... a peculiar people; 1 Peter 2:9
Israel: And ye shall be unto me a kingdom of priests, and an holy nation. Exodus 19:6	**The Church:** A royal priesthood, a holy nation. 1 Peter 2:9
Israel: But ye shall destroy their (the pagans) altars, break their images, and cut down their groves Exodus 34:13 (Israel should subdue the pagans)	The woman standing on the moon. Revelation 12:1 (A picture of the Church standing over paganism)

Chart No 6 -Israel in the Wilderness Compared with the Woman in the Wilderness

Israel	The Woman
In the wilderness God gave them bread from heaven, to feed them. Exodus 16:4	God prepares a place in the wilderness to feed the woman. Revelation 12:6
Out of Egypt, God bare them on eagle's wings, to bring Israel into the wilderness unto himself. Exodus 19:4	And to the woman was given two wings of a great eagle, that she might fly into the wilderness. Revelation 12:14
Israel was attacked by Amalek, Satan's people. **(War in the Wilderness)** Exodus 17:8	And the dragon (Satan) was wrath with the woman, and went to make war with the remnant of her seed. **(War in the wilderness)** Revelation 12:17
The earth opened her mouth to swallow up the wicked, those who almost caused the total destruction of Israel. Numbers 16:1 & 32	Satan will inspire a flood of the wicked to carry away (that is, destroy) the woman, but the earth will open her mouth to swallow up those wicked. Revelation 12:15 & 16.
Israel in the Wilderness was attacked by serpents. Numbers 21:6-7	The dragon, that old serpent, will attack the woman. Revelation 12:13-15
The Exodus generation perished in the wilderness Numbers 21:6 & Hebrews 3:17	The woman will perish in the wilderness. Compare Revelation 12:17 with 13:7 and Daniel 7:25

real bread of heaven. The bread which came down from heaven for Israel was a type of the Lord Jesus. It foreshadowed his ministry as the one who would give eternal life.

Another example; God said that if Israel would obey his voice they would be to God a kingdom of priests, a holy nation (Exodus 19:6). One day on earth Israel will obtain these promises. Yet the Church is already such a priesthood, a holy nation (1 Peter 2:9). Therefore the Church obtained an office for which Israel now has to wait. Again in Isaiah 66:7-8; we read of a 'man-child' being brought forth by the earth (refer to the chapter '**The Other Man-Child**'). Out of the earth comes forth a group of resurrected saints. This group of resurrected saints is called a 'man-child'. In Revelation 12:6 there is a second 'man-child', but this time it comes forth out of a heavenly woman. As was already shown in this study, the 'man-child' out of the earth represents the resurrected saints of Israel, while the 'man-child' out of the heavenly woman represents the church, the body of Christ. On both occasions at first glance Scripture appears to refer to the same event. This is because Israel and the Church are so closely related. It is only when we take a closer look that the important differences can be discovered which make it clear that two different events at different times are in view. Once this is understood, it will help us in the future to be able to distinguish between Israel, the earthly covenant people and the Church with her heavenly destiny. This principle can also be seen when comparing Israel in the wilderness with the woman of Revelation 12.

There are many similarities between the two, which help us to obtain a better understanding of the prophecy in Revelation 12. What had its precedence in the wilderness on earth, helps us to understand better what the sign of the woman in the sky is meant to convey. Israel's experience gives us a clue to understand the woman of Revelation 12. Let us first consider the similarities between the two. See Chart No 5 on page 147.

Israel's Exodus generation is a type of the woman of Revelation 12. God gave promises to Israel and had they been obedient, the whole nation could have enjoyed them. Likewise God gave promises to the Church. These promises could be enjoyed by every church-goer, if all were born again. We can therefore see that Israel is a type of the woman. Now let us see if Israel's Exodus generation (those who died in the wilderness) compares with the woman in the wilderness.

God determined that the parents of Israel, which formed the larger part of the assembly (all those over 20 years), would not make it to the promised land. Only their children, the smaller part of the assembly (those under 20 years) would inherit the land. Hence out of the larger group of people was separated a smaller group of people, just as in Revelation 12 where the smaller group of true believers comes out of the larger group, the visible Church.

The larger body was doomed to perish in the wilderness, while the smaller body departed later to inherit the promises. This is also what will happen to the woman and her child. The woman representing the visible Church is the larger body of people. The true Church, which at the rapture is separated from the woman, is the smaller body of people. After the woman gives birth to the child she finds herself in the wilderness where she is fed by the providence of God, just as Israel was fed by God.

The woman is attacked by Satan the serpent; Israel was attacked by serpents. The woman (the remains of the visible Church) will face war in the wilderness (Revelation 12:17); Israel faced war in the wilderness (Exodus 17:8). Satan will inspire a flood of the wicked to totally do away with (destroy) the woman, but the earth will open her mouth and swallow them up. Satan, likewise, inspired a multitude of the wicked to oppose Moses and therefore God. This almost resulted in the total destruction of Israel, but the earth opened her mouth and swallowed them up, (Numbers Chapter 16). Again the woman will perish in the wilderness. Likewise Israel's rebellious generation also perished in the wilderness. **Refer to Chart No 6 on page 148.**

Finally, many of the remnant of the visible Church will die as saved persons, they are Tribulation saints. Likewise many of Israel's Exodus generation who died would have been saved persons. All this indicates that Israel in the wilderness is a type of the woman in Revelation 12. Consequently by comparing the woman with Israel's Exodus generation we can gain some additional truth about the woman.

If it is accepted that old Israel is a type, a forerunner, of the woman in Revelation 12, then it must be accepted that Israel cannot be that woman, because all of Israel's Exodus generation (a type of the woman in the wilderness) died with the exception of two. Hence the woman or the remnant of the visible Church must likewise all die in the wilderness. Now if Israel represented that woman, then all of future Israel would also have to die in the wilderness. But we know that this is impossible, since Israel is going to inherit the earthly kingdom of God. So for this reason alone Israel cannot be the woman of Revelation chapter 12.

Until now we have concentrated mainly on Israel's Exodus generation and compared it with the woman in the wilderness. But compare Israel's new generation with those who came out of the wilderness, and compare them with the 'man-child', who came out of the woman. If the Exodus generation compares with the woman, perhaps the generation of the book of Joshua compares with the 'man-child', the raptured Church.

The war for the promised land was fought on two levels. Joshua and his army fought in the physical realm, but the captain of the heavenly host helped them in the spiritual realm. When the Church is raptured the heavenly host will also help her. A war is fought in heaven to protect the saints.

Just as the promised land had to be cleansed and cleared from the pagan Satan worshippers, likewise the heavenlies will have to be cleansed and vacated of Satan's host.

The promises which the whole nation of Israel had received were only inherited by the new generation. The previous generation missed out; they never made it to the promised land. Likewise, many of the spiritual blessings and purposes which were given to the whole Church will not be enjoyed by the whole Church, but only by the true Church which will be raptured. **Refer to Chart No 7 on the next page.**

Now it appears that indeed Israel's new generation is a type of the 'man-child'. Both are groups of saved people. If this is so, then it would confirm the view expressed in this study that the 'man-child' is the Church, the body of Christ, and not the baby Jesus. For this reason the woman in heaven cannot be Israel.

Chart No 7 -Israel's New Generation compared with the Man Child

Israel's Exodus Generation	The Man Child
The host of heaven fought for Israel (in the spiritual realm against satanic forces), while Israel began to inherit the promised land. Joshua 5:13-14 & 23:3	The host of heaven will fight against Satan's host, while the Church inherit their position in heaven. Revelation 12:7
The promised land had to be cleansed from all pagans (Satan's people), to prepare the land for God's people. Joshua 3:10 & 13:6-7	The heavens will be cleansed from Satan and his angels, to prepare them for God's saints. Revelation 12:8
Israel entered the promised land by a miracle (Jordan river dried up). Joshua 3:1-17	The Church will enter heaven by a miracle (the rapture). 1 Thessalonians 4:15-17
God's people replaced Satan's people, in the promised land. Deuteronomy 20:16 & 17	The raptured Church replaces Satan's host in the heavenlies. Revelation 12:5 & 8
Only Israel's new generation inherited the land and the promises which were given to all Israel. The Exodus generation missed out.	Only the true Church will inherit all spiritual promises given to the whole Church. The visible Church will miss many.

Israel Does Not Represent the Woman of Revelation 12

We now investigate whether or not Israel fits the description of the woman with the 'man-child'. Most of the time Israel did not overcome pagan religions, but copied the sun and moon worship of the pagan nations around them (2 Kings 23:5, Jeremiah 8:2). Therefore it cannot be said that Israel subdued pagan religions, rather it was often the other way around. Israel took on paganism for itself. And so the sign of the woman having the moon under her feet does not, for this reason alone, fit the nation of Israel.

The child was caught up to God and to his throne. Jesus was never caught up. He 'ascended' to heaven about 33 years later. The context of Revelation 12:5 strongly indicates that the child, after its birth, was immediately caught up to heaven. There is no indication of a gap of 33 years. If the Lord Jesus Christ is in view here, then why is the Cross, which is the most important part of his earthly ministry, not mentioned in connection with the 'man-child'?

If the woman represents Israel, which gave birth to the 'man-child' then when, before the birth of Christ, did Israel experience the birth pangs in relation to the forthcoming child, which must have happened if we insist that Israel is the woman of Revelation chapter 12? History does not record any such events.

The dragon stood before the woman to devour the child as soon as it was born. But Herod's attempt to kill the child Christ Jesus happened about 2 years later, not immediately. Also if the child would have been killed, it would not have been devoured. To kill someone or to devour him are two different things.

Nothing happened to Israel after the birth of Christ, which would correspond to the experience of the woman in Revelation 12. Israel did not have to flee into the wilderness after the birth of Christ, nor was a place prepared for her. If Israel was the woman, then there has to be a gap of about 2,000 years between the end of verse five and the beginning of verse six. But there is nothing whatsoever written to indicate such a gap.

If Israel is in fact the woman of Revelation 12, then when have they fled, or when will they flee into the wilderness? This question can't be avoided, because if Israel never fulfils this prophetic requirement then Israel cannot represent the woman of Revelation 12. If Israel's whereabouts can be traced, and it is concluded that they will as a whole remain in their own land, then any other argument why Israel must be the woman becomes superfluous. It is a known fact of history that until now Israel was never fed for 3½ years in the wilderness. Therefore if Israel is going to fulfil that prophetic condition it must happen in the future, and it must happen during or after the Tribulation. Fortunately we are able to trace Israel's whereabouts during the Tribulation and afterwards, by studying the Olivet discourse and related Scriptures.

Israel will be in their land during the first half of their Tribulation, since they will witness the setting up of the abomination which causes desolation (Matthew 24:15). That event happens 3½ years after the beginning of the Tribulation. Also the context of the Olivet discourse makes it clear that the Jews will be in their own land during that time. During the second half of Israel's Tribulation, which is the time of Jacob's trouble, Israel likewise must be in their land for the following reasons:

1. If they would have fled into the wilderness into a relatively safe place, it could not be called the time of Jacob's trouble. The time of this great Tribulation will be the worst time Israel has ever experienced.

2. The Jews must be in their own land during the time of their Tribulation. The Lord speaking about the end time Jewish believers said in Matthew 10:23 that when persecuted they should flee to other cities. But before they could travel through every city in Israel. The Lord would have come back. This makes it clear that the bulk of the Jews have to be in their own land right up to the time of the Lord's return to the mount of Olives.

3. Zechariah 14:1-4; speaks about the time of Israel's trouble. The context leaves little doubt that the end of their Tribulation is in view. And the Jews are in Jerusalem. Therefore Israel is seen to be in their own land right up to the second coming, and can hardly be

hiding away in some wilderness place at the same time.

Also the woman of Revelation 12 is said to fly in to the wilderness to her place. This in today's language would suggest an airlift. While it should present no problem for the remnant of the woman during the early part of the Tribulation, to arrange such an airlift for Israel during the latter part or after their Tribulation would be a very different prospect. During the Tribulation, but especially afterwards during the interval, world conditions will make such an airlift an impossibility. Industry, and with it air travel, will not function after the world has experienced all those predicted upheavals.

Therefore it is concluded that prophecy gives Israel no time to spend 3½ years in the wilderness. For this reason, the view that Israel represents the woman of Revelation chapter 12 has again to be rejected.

Revelation is a book which deals primarily with the Church and the Gentiles. This is immediately established in Revelation chapters one and two, and is also confirmed in the last chapter. It is stated that Jesus Christ has given this Revelation to show to his servants things which must shortly come to pass. At the time John was given the vision and wrote the book, the nation of Israel no longer existed and the *servants* to which the Lord referred were Christians. Again in chapter 22:16 we read, "*I Jesus have sent mine angel to testify unto you these things in the churches*", thus making it evident that the book of Revelation was given primarily for the churches. Hence any event in the book of Revelation should be interpreted as affecting mainly the Gentiles, unless the context demands otherwise.

For this reason if the text refers to Israel, it must be clearly indicated, as it is done in regard to the 144,000 servants of chapter seven. If there is no clear reference to Israel, it should be assumed that the text deals with the Church or the Gentiles. Since chapter 12 does not mention Israel at all, we should seek to find the woman's role in connection with the Church.

Throughout the Bible when symbols are used in prophecy they are only used to record events which are still future at the time of writing. Past events are always recorded literally. Since the birth of Christ was a past event by the time John wrote the book of Revelation, he would not have resorted to symbolical language if he wanted to describe an event in connection with the birth of Christ, specially since Revelation 1:19 makes it clear that only three times are to be considered.

1. "***The things which thou hast seen***"; these refer to John's vision of Jesus Christ in chapter one.

2. "***The things which are***"; these were the things taking place at the time of John's writing.

3. "***The things which shall be***"; these would be the future events from John's point of time.

Therefore past events like the birth of Christ are not considered in the book of Revelation.

Joseph's Dream

The dream of Joseph (Genesis 37:9-10) is always presented as proof that the sun and the moon are symbolic for Israel, and hence the woman of Revelation chapter 12 must represent Israel.

"*And he dreamed yet another dream, and told it his brethren, and said, Behold, I have dreamed a dream more; and, behold, the sun and the moon and the eleven stars made obeisance to me. And he told it to his father, and to his brethren: and his father rebuked him, and said unto him, What is this dream that thou hast dreamed? Shall I and thy mother and thy brethren indeed come to bow down ourselves to thee to the earth?*"

The interpretation normally follows along these lines: The sun represents Jacob, the moon Rachel the mother of Joseph and the 11 stars represent the 12 sons of Jacob. Whatever message this dream was meant to deliver is probably a study in itself. However to claim that because of this dream the woman of Revelation 12 has to be Israel is not possible. Let's apply the symbols, as they are understood by those who say that Israel represents the woman of Revelation 12, and fit them into the vision of Revelation 12.

1. Jacob represents the sun. This would mean that the woman (if she represents Israel) is clothed with whatever Jacob symbolises. Was it ever said of Jacob that he was the light of the world? The symbol does not fit.

2. Rachel represents the moon. This interpretation is even worse. Since in this case Israel is said to be standing on her mother (the woman standing on the moon). It makes no sense.

3. The 11 stars which Joseph saw in his dream represent the 12 sons of Jacob. There is an obvious mathematical error in this explanation. How can the 11 stars which Joseph saw, all of a sudden become 12 stars? Even if there was no discrepancy, how can one connect the 12 sons of Jacob with a crown which the woman wears? Where is the significance? How could that jealous bunch of brothers symbolise royalty and glory? Careful analysis should make it clear that Joseph's dream cannot be used to prove that the woman of Revelation 12 represents Israel.

For all the above reasons it is here concluded that Israel does not represent the woman of Revelation chapter 12.

Can Mary be the Queen of Heaven?

There are those who say that Mary is the queen of heaven. If this is so, then she must represent the woman of Revelation chapter 12, and must fit the picture better than the Church, otherwise that claim is not true. Does Mary fit the facts as set out in that chapter? Since we have already shown, verse by verse, that the Church fits the description of Revelation chapter 12 we shall not deal with every verse but merely point out only those verses where there are problems if Mary is to be queen of heaven. Also we shall disregard any claim that Mary is the queen of heaven which is based upon tradition. The word of God alone should be our authority in all matters.

The doctrine that Mary is the queen of Heaven runs into similar problems as the teaching that Israel represents that woman. If Mary is the woman and Jesus the man-child, then there is a problem in verse four. Satan's attempt on the life of the child Jesus did not happen as soon as he was born. But certainly later, up to two years. Again, Christ was not immediately caught up to heaven as was pointed out previously, but he ascended about 33 years later. Therefore these facts contradict the claim that Mary is the queen of heaven.

In verse five it is stated that the man-child was caught up to heaven, to the throne of God. It is the child not the woman which is taken up to the throne of God. In fact the woman loses even her elevated position in the sky once the man-child is born. How can all this possibly be connected to Mary?

What about verse six? Where in the Bible is it recorded that Mary had to flee for 3½ years into the wilderness where people fed her? Nothing at all is mentioned, the Bible is silent. It is not correct to use one verse of Scripture which lends itself for an interpretation, if the rest of the word of God keeps silent, or even contradicts the interpretation.

Again, verses seven and eight mention the war in heaven immediately after the man-child was caught up to heaven and the woman had to flee into the wilderness. How can that war be connected with Mary? As a result of that war Satan is cast out of heaven onto the earth (Revelation 12:13). Hence as all this would have to have happened soon after the birth of the man-child, Satan would today be confined to the earth, and in that case he could no longer be said to be the prince of the air. Yet according to Ephesians 2:2 it is from the air where Satan still operates today.

The events of verse 10 follow soon after the birth of the man-child. It is stated that Satan has been cast down to earth and that the kingdom of God has come in strength and power. If Mary had brought forth the man-child, then this kingdom should be in place today. Where is the evidence of this? Is Satan with his demonic forces bound (which according to Revelation 20:2-3; he will be) when God's kingdom has been set up on earth? There is no evidence of this either.

In verse 12 it is stated that the Devil is come down to the earth with great wrath, because he knows that he has but a short time left. Since this, as has already been pointed out, has to happen shortly after the birth of the man-child, then the short time of verse 12 has turned out to be a time span of 2,000 years. Obviously the claim that Mary is the queen of heaven does not tie up with the Scriptures.

Verse 13; Is there any record that Mary was ever persecuted? There is no record of this in the Bible.

Verse 14; When did Mary fly into the wilderness for 3½ years?

If Mary is the woman, then who are the remnant of her seed? These which are the remnant must also like the man-child have come forth out of the woman, they must naturally be brothers and sisters of the man-child. Since they have the same mother, they must be related, and must be of the same kind. But those who claim that Mary is the woman deny that Mary ever had other children. If so, then who are those which have come forth out of this woman? If the man-child is to be the baby Jesus, that is, God in a human body, then who are those which also came out of the woman?

If it is assumed that Mary is the queen of heaven and that she rules as queen in the heavenlies, then what about the statement of Scripture that Christ Jesus is Lord of lords, and King of kings (Revelation 19:16). Surley if words mean anything, then it means that Christ is ruling, not his earthly mother. It is the same situation as one currently existing here on earth. As long as the queen of England sits on her throne, her son Prince Charles cannot be king. Likewise in heaven if the son rules, then his mother cannot rule at the same time. Mother and son cannot rule at the same time. The Church will rule only as a helpmeet, because she is the wife of the King. We have seen that the Scriptures indicate that the Church will be the wife of Christ, and as such she could be a heavenly queen. Therefore Mary cannot also be a queen of heaven.

However Scripture does mention another queen of heaven, a false queen, Satan's fake queen. We read about her in Jeremiah 7:18; 44:17-19 and Revelation 18:7. It is every individual's own responsibility to make sure they know and understand the truth. First and foremost you should consider only that which the word of God itself proclaims, because it is your eternal destiny which is at stake. You alone are responsible before God, therefore it is important to fully understand that salvation is first and foremost through the word of God in conjunction with the Holy Spirit, and not that of man, or of tradition. Anyone whose name is not written in the Lamb's book of life will not be able to point the finger at, or blame, any other person for their eternal state. It is our own personal responsibility.